The Complete Lodge Secretary

The Complete Lodge Secretary

Gordon G. Hunt

The Complete Lodge Secretary
Gordon Hunt

First published 2010

ISBN 978 0 85318 327 3

Published by Lewis Masonic

an imprint of Ian Allan Publishing Ltd, Hersham, Surrey KT12 4RG.
Printed in England by Ian Allan Printing Ltd, Hersham, Surrey KT12 4RG.

Visit the Ian Allan Publishing website at www.ianallanpublishing.com

Distributed in the United States of America and Canada by BookMasters Distribution Services.

Biography

Gordon G. Hunt was initiated into Craft Masonry in the St. Anselm Lodge No. 5166 of Chester in 1976 and became Master in 1983. Following a move to London, he joined Archimedean Lodge No. 3613 in 1988 and became Master in 1990 and again in 2004. In 1992 he was appointed Secretary of Archimedean Lodge, a post he held for eight years and was again appointed Secretary in 2008, an office he still holds. He was honoured with London Grand Rank in 1999 and promoted to Senior London Grand Rank in 2009. Also in 2009 he was appointed Senior Warden of Halsey Lodge No. 1479 of St Albans.

He has been First Principal of two Royal Arch Chapters in London, and he currently holds the office of Scribe E of Duke of Cornwall Chapter No. 1839.

He is active in other Masonic Orders in London and Hertfordshire including holding the office of Registrar in The Military Lodges Preceptory No. 300.

During his first period as Lodge Secretary Gordon Hunt designed and developed "The Complete Lodge Secretary" computer program that was first released in 1997. It was subsequently updated and re-launched in 2006 with updates in 2007 and 2008. The bespoke program, which is founded on a data base, dynamically incorporates the wording of the rules of the Book of Constitutions and Points of Procedure from "Information for the Guidance of Members of the Craft".

"The Complete Lodge Secretary" computer program centralises Lodge information, provides reports when and where needed, or exports, if required, to MS Office programs. It ensures that all membership and Lodge information is entered only once and provides continuity by making Lodge history and advice immediately accessible when a new Secretary takes office. It is the concepts and structure of the program that inspired the book *The Complete Lodge Secretary.*

Foreword

I first met Brother Gordon G. Hunt some five years ago, when he made an appointment to see me and demonstrate a computer program he had developed to assist the Lodge Secretary. Despite my initial scepticism (receiving approaches from Brethren or suppliers with new ideas is an occupational hazard for me), it did not take me many minutes to recognise that what he was showing me was the real thing – a genuinely helpful program that would take much of the drudgery and risk out of the Secretary's job. I was glad to be able to help in a small way by helping him obtain the permission of the Board of General Purposes to reproduce in the program pertinent extracts from the Book of Constitutions and edicts of Grand Lodge. The program, The Complete Lodge Secretary, has been selling steadily over the intervening years.

I was therefore delighted to be approached by Brother Hunt with the text of this book, which provides in written form the same rigorous analysis of the processes which a Secretary must follow as has already been amply demonstrated in the computer program. I am confident that the book, with its greater accessibility and portability, will prove no less valuable a guide to Lodge Secretaries than its electronic predecessor, and I commend it to readers.

Graham Redman

January 2010

Preface

I first became a Lodge Secretary in 1992, an office I held for eight years. Then, as now, my objective was to enjoy the job and perform it to the best of my ability.

Coming from the background of quantity surveying I was already familiar with the discipline of working within defined sets of rules and standards and delivering to firm deadlines (Contracts, Methods of Measurement, Tenders and Project Schedules). I was also heavily committed to using computers as tools on a daily basis as a member of a profession that spent much of its time number crunching and data processing. By the late 1970s I had applied this commitment to computer system development.

Therefore, it is not surprising that on becoming a Lodge Secretary, my mindset looked upon Lodges, Meetings and Members as data and the Book of Constitutions as the Rules and Standards by which the data must be managed. Consequently, I set about looking for and developing computing solutions to assist in the Lodge Secretarial role.

The outcome was a computer program, built around the Rules of the *Book of Constitutions*, initially for my own use but later (as others saw the program), I was encouraged to make it generally available. In 1997 **The Complete Lodge Secretary** computer program was launched.

In 2006, I was fortunate enough to obtain Grand Lodge permission* to incorporate within the program the wording of the *Book of Constitutions* and *Information for the Guidance of Members of the Craft*. A new version of **The Complete Lodge Secretary** was launched incorporating new technology, improved graphics and updated Rules and Guidance. **The Complete Lodge Secretary** program was commercially available through Lewis Masonic, amongst others.

In 2008, Lewis Masonic suggested that the format of the program might lend itself as a book for Lodge Secretaries. I found this suggestion at once challenging, appealing and daunting.

It was challenging because I had, by serendipity, planning and inevitability, once more become Secretary of a Craft Lodge, Scribe E of a Royal Arch Chapter and Registrar of a KT Preceptory all within a 12-month period, each of which would add to my experience but would also impact significantly on my available time.

It was appealing because it aligned with my own view that there was a pressing need for a book to address how new technologies, methods of communication and the consequent changes adopted by Provinces and Grand Lodge fitted in with the traditional role of a Lodge Secretary.

It was daunting because I knew that Lodge Secretaries were amongst the most experienced and dedicated of Masons, many of whom had been proficiently fulfilling the Secretarial role for many years. Also, I knew that my knowledge and interpretation of the Rules of the *Book of Constitutions* and *Information for the Guidance of Members of the Craft* would have to align with those of Grand Lodge if my book was to carry any credibility.

In the end the challenge and the appeal were too great for me to resist, and the book *The Complete Lodge Secretary* became a reality.

In writing this book, I attempted to take a pragmatic approach by linking

- the reality, anomalies and serendipity of life,
- the rectitude of the Rules and Regulations of the Book of Constitutions,
- the knowledge, judgement and wisdom of the Lodge Secretary and
- the sophistication, exponential growth and ubiquitous intrusion of computers and communications system technologies.

It is my hope that the book will prove useful and interesting to both new and existing Secretaries alike.

* * *

* Within The Complete Lodge Secretary computer program, extracts from the *Book of Constitutions* are reproduced by kind permission of the Board of General Purposes of the United Grand Lodge of England. The manner in which they are applied is the sole responsibility of Lodge Software Ltd.

Acknowledgements

I wish to acknowledge those without whom *The Complete Lodge Secretary* would not have been produced. Firstly for the patience and support of my partner, Angie, who saw precious little of me for large parts of 2009 whilst I was working on the book.

For the introductions effected by Brother Peter Boughton and Brother George Souter resulting in my meeting with Brother David Allan of Ian Allan Publishing, who have published the book.

For Brother Andrew Croci, Head of Registration Section at Grand Lodge who gave guidance on Chapter 5 - Grand Lodge, Metropolitan, Provincial & District Grand Lodge and for Brother Richard Gan, Deputy Grand Secretary of the Grand Lodge of Mark Master Masons for his proof reading and constructive final editing.

Finally, I wish to record my appreciation for the invaluable assistance of Brother Graham Redman, Assistant Grand Secretary, for his time spent reading the book; for providing helpful guidance, particularly for clarification in the interpretation of sections of the Book of Constitutions and especially for agreeing to contribute the Foreword to this book.

CONTENTS

CHAPTER 1

DEFINING THE ROLE OF THE LODGE SECRETARY

1.1 Introduction
1.2 Communication
1.3 Information, Knowledge and Wisdom
1.4 Organisations, People and Events

1.1 Introduction

The Complete Lodge Secretary is intended to assist Lodge Secretaries in fulfilling their role in the 21st Century.

It addresses the fundamental attributes of knowledge, wisdom and judgement required of every Lodge Secretary.

It also considers the impact made on the Secretary's role by the ubiquitous computer and the exponential growth and development of communications technologies.

When methodologies are subject to change, it is right to take account of the balance between the benefits that new systems bring and the perceived or real detrimental factors that arise in consequence of the changes. This balance is recognised by, and sometimes influences, the rate of change.

Freemasonry is never quick to change, which is one of its attractions to the majority of members. However, Grand Lodge and Metropolitan, Provincial and District Grand Lodges are progressively changing their approach by adopting the new technologies to assist with the communication and dissemination of information to the membership.

It seems evident that three of the key priorities of Grand Lodge that affect how the Secretary fulfils the duties of his office are:-

- Communication with its membership
- Recording and reporting of details, progress and status of Lodge Members.
- Compliance with the Rules and edicts passed by Grand Lodge.

In *The Complete Lodge Secretary* addressing the basic role of the Secretary is paramount together with the rules and guidelines within which he is bound to work.

Recognising the new tools that are available to assist the Secretary in his role is a secondary consideration. However, it is impossible to ignore the phenomenal growth of new methods of communication and their impact.

1.2 Communication

The Role of the Lodge Secretary can best be defined as one of communicating Information, Knowledge and Wisdom relating to People, Organisations and Events.

Thirty years ago, in 1980, 'Telex' ticker tape was still in use but there were no commercial fax machines, no portable computers, no mobile telephones, no text messages, no commercial emails, no Internet, no GPS navigation. It is very different today!

Along with the rest of the world, the Lodge Secretary has to choose which of the available tools and technologies he wishes to adopt and when.

His alternative methods for communicating are:-

Person To Person – This is the area where the Lodge Secretary initially proves his worth and continues to demonstrate the excellent qualities described more fully later. In most instances it is his interpersonal skills, authority and Masonic knowledge that lead a Master to appoint a brother as Secretary.

Letter – The traditional and effective way of communicating, no longer the quickest and generally considered as the most formal method. Some parts of the Constitution require recorded or registered letters.

Fax – This is still occasionally useful but it is now more common to email copies of 'scanned' documents.

Phone – There is seldom a valid excuse for not being able to make telephone contact (to or from the Secretary) via mobile phones, voice mail, text messages, land lines, answer-phones and pagers.

Email – Increasingly the most common form of communication, emails are less formal than letters. They have the benefit of being able to send many letters, with document attachments, instantly and at no cost. They also have disadvantages, such as potentially sending to the wrong person, not always being sure it has arrived, being unsure if it has been deleted as 'Spam' and people frequently changing email addresses. (See Chapters 4.3 and 12.5)

Lodge Website – An increasing number of Lodges have their own Web Site containing general information. Some also have a 'Member's Room' with password access that enables members to communicate – including confirming attendance at Lodge.

1.3 Information, Knowledge and Wisdom

Information

The Secretary generally becomes the repository of information relating to the Lodge and its members, sent or communicated to him from many sources.

The core information available to the Secretary is extensive and he has to decide whether to turn it into knowledge that will later be applied with wisdom or to communicate the information direct to those who need to receive it. Included in this information are the following:-

- United Grand Lodge of England Constitutions
- Information for the Guidance of Members of the Craft
- Lodge by-laws
- Copy of Grand Lodge forms, returns and notices
- Metropolitan/Provincial/District forms and notices
- Incoming and outgoing correspondence
- Any other items for reference at Risings
- Lodge Meeting minutes
- Lodge attendance records
- Lodge Committee minutes
- Secretarial expenses

Knowledge

The Secretary has to gain a comprehensive knowledge of the many areas affecting his job. Depending upon how long he has been in Freemasonry, this can be quite a steep learning curve.

- Knowledge of Lodge procedures
- Understanding and interpretation of rules
- Knowledge of lead times
- Recording, administering and delivering all Information
- Knowledge of and familiarity with Members

Wisdom

Having and applying wisdom comes as a consequence of knowledge, experience and good judgement. With wisdom comes calm and confidence, the beneficial effects of which will be felt in the Lodge.

- Assisting the Master in delivering a happy Lodge.
- Striking balance between authority, help and support.

1.4 Organisations, People and Events

Organisations

The Organisations that the Secretary will encounter and communicate with include the following:-

- Grand Lodge
- Metropolitan, Provincial and District Grand Lodges
- Other Lodges
- Secretary's own Lodge
- Service providers

People

The people that the Secretary will communicate and deal with are listed below. In many ways, each of the following categories has distinctive characteristics.

- Officers of Grand Lodge
- Officers of Metropolitan, Provincial and District Grand Lodges
- Members of other Lodges
- Members of Secretary's Lodge
- Relatives of Members
- Past and future Members
- Service providers
- The general public

Events

The Secretary will be either directly involved in or will communicate with promoters, organisers and attendees at the following events.

- Grand Lodge meetings
- Metropolitan, Provincial and District meetings
- Metropolitan, Provincial and District training sessions
- Lodge meetings
- Lodges of instruction
- General purpose/permanent committee meetings
- Social gatherings
- Charity events.

CHAPTER 2

THE SECRETARY'S ROLE AND DUTIES

2.1 Generally
2.2 Defined Duties
2.3 Undefined Qualities and Responsibilities

2.1 Generally

The role of the Lodge Secretary is determined by the following:

1. The Book of Constitutions
2. Information for the Guidance of Members of the Craft
3. The Lodge By-laws
4. Other roles and duties emanating from the position of Lodge Secretary and thereby the chief administrator of the Lodge.

For purposes of clarity in this chapter, the first three activities have been identified as 'Defined Duties' and the fourth as 'Undefined Qualities and Responsibilities'.

2.2 Defined Duties

The Secretary is specifically referred to in the *Book of Constitutions*, the *Information for the Guidance of Members of the Craft* and the Lodge by-laws. These three documents set down the Rules that the Lodge and its Members must adhere to and observe. Each of these references is listed briefly below as an aid to the Secretary in understanding of the defined scope of his responsibilities.

2.2.1 Book of Constitutions

The following table identifies where the Secretary is specifically mentioned in the Book of Constitutions (B of C). The wording in quotations is an abbreviated extract that shows the context. However, the full Rule should be referred to in practice.

Rule / Location	B of C Subheading	Requirement of Secretary
Page vii	Antient Charges and Regulations	"ANTIENT CHARGES AND REGULATIONS to be read by the *Secretary*… to the Master Elect prior to his Installation in the Chair of the Lodge."
47	To whom business papers and reports to be transmitted	The Lodge *Secretary*, recorded as such in the Annual List of Members (Rule 151) will receive two copies of business papers (Quarterly Communications etc) from Grand Lodge. "On receipt of these copies the *Secretary* shall immediately forward one of them to the Master of the Lodge".
104(a)	Officers of a Lodge	"The regular Officers of a Lodge shall be the Master and his two Wardens, a Treasurer, a *Secretary*… additional officers…may include…an Assistant *Secretary*..."
104(c)		"A Lodge in its by-laws may provide that the services of its *Secretary* be equivalent to the appropriate subscription to the Lodge..."
104(d)		"The Officers of a Lodge shall take precedence for investiture and otherwise in the following order: Master, Senior Warden, Junior Warden, Chaplain (if any), Treasurer, *Secretary*, Director of Ceremonies (if any)…
105(a)	Election and Installation of Master	"If there be only one nomination and if no other member duly qualified shall have indicated to the *Secretary* that he wishes to be considered … it shall be permissible for the Master to declare the election…"
105(b)		"A motion to this effect shall be entertained ...only if written notice … shall have been given to the *Secretary*...
		"... the proposed motion and of the separate statement shall be forwarded...to the Master Elect by the *Secretary*, and a copy of the proposed motion, but not a copy of the separate statement, shall be printed on the summons …"

144	Minutes	"Every Lodge shall keep a Minute Book in which the Master or the *Secretary* shall regularly enter from time to time…"
146(i)	Annual Return of Members	"Every Lodge, by its *Secretary*, shall … transmit to the Grand *Secretary*, ...a return of the persons, who were during such year its subscribing members."
		"Such returns shall be signed by the Master and the *Secretary*."
151	Annual Installation Return	"Every Lodge, by its *Secretary*, shall annually, immediately after the installation of the Master, make a return to the Grand *Secretary* of the Master, Wardens…" "The Master and *Secretary* shall sign the return."
159	Candidates for Initiation	"The particulars required of the candidate… shall be furnished to the *Secretary* of the Lodge, previously to the meeting ...at which the proposal is to be made…"
160	Initiation in cases of urgency	"...the candidate… to furnish the appropriate particulars to the *Secretary*... on the printed form of application mentioned in Rule 159,"
163(b)	Joining Members	"The particulars required of the candidate… shall be furnished to the *Secretary* of the Lodge, previously to the meeting ...at which the proposal is to be made…"
163(c)	Certificate to be produced	"...the candidate must produce to the *Secretary* of the Lodge his Grand Lodge Certificate...and…a certificate of good standing from each of the Lodges of which he is a member…"
163(e)	Joining Members from other Jurisdictions	"…the *Secretary*… shall...apply to the Grand *Secretary*... to ascertain that the Grand Lodge under which the Brother was initiated is recognised …"
164(a)(i)	Election of candidates for initiation or joining	"…If the Candidate is...Initiated... joins or rejoins the Lodge, the form shall immediately be signed by the *Secretary* and sent… to the Grand *Secretary*…"

164(a)(ii)		"...A candidate's proposer or seconder, or the *Secretary* of the Lodge, who knowingly makes or leaves uncorrected such a false statement shall be liable to the same penalty..."
164(c)		"...Lodge to specify in its by-laws that ... particulars of a candidate...be deposited with the *Secretary* for a reasonable number of days before the meeting at which the candidate is to be proposed... "
165A(b)	Transfer of membership on Amalgamation	"...joint Registration Form...appended thereto a certificate signed by the Master and *Secretary* of the Amalgamating Lodge that none of the Brethren therein named is indebted to the Lodge..."
165A(c)		"(c) the joint Registration Form shall be transmitted to the *Secretary* of the continuing Lodge ..."
173(a)	Conferment of degrees by request	"No Lodge ... shall pass or raise a Brother who has been initiated in another Lodge except at the written request of the Master ... and the *Secretary* of the Lodge in which he was initiated."
174(d)	Presentation of Certificate	A Brother's Grand Lodge Certificate should be presented to him in open Lodge, and the fact entered on the minutes, but ... where this cannot conveniently be done, the Certificate shall be sent ...by registered post, and the *Secretary* shall report the fact at the next regular meeting.
183	Resignation	"A member ... may at any time ...resign his membership by notifying such resignation either by a written notice to the *Secretary* or orally to the Lodge ... If the resignation be so notified to the *Secretary*, he shall communicate it to the Lodge at the next regular meeting...the resignation...if notified to the *Secretary* and reported to the Lodge, takes effect from the time such notification...was received by the *Secretary*..."
187(iv)	Regulations to be observed by Lodges in the jurisdiction of a new Sovereign Grand Lodge	"Immediately after such meeting a full copy of the minutes and a list from the signature book of all members attending, together with the numbers voting for or against, shall be sent to the Grand *Secretary*, verified under the hand of the presiding Master, and countersigned by the *Secretary* of the Lodge."

2.2.2 Information for the Guidance of Members of the Craft

The booklet entitled *Information for the Guidance of Members of the Craft* is issued with each copy of the *Book of Constitutions* and presented to each Candidate at his Initiation and each Master at his Installation.

Its 'Points of Procedure' carry the full weight as edicts from the Board of General Purposes of the United Grand Lodge of England. It can therefore be taken as an extension to the *Book of Constitutions* and should be read in conjunction with it.

The following 'Points of Procedure' specifically mention the **Secretary** within the text.

Emoluments to Lodge Officers

Rule 104 of the *Book of Constitutions* permits for the inclusion in the by-laws of a Lodge of a provision for the remission of the Lodge subscription of the **Secretary**. It follows that it would be ultra vires to include in the by-laws any provision for the remission of the subscriptions payable by any member of the Lodge other than the **Secretary**...

Lodge Minutes

The Board has given consideration also to the use of loose attendance sheets to ... the Signature or Attendance book. The Board is of the opinion that the requirements of the second part of Rule 144, *Book of Constitutions*, are met if these sheets are irremovably affixed to the Minutes of the meeting to which they refer, provided that each sheet is initialled by the Master or **Secretary**.

... It follows from this that no valid objection can be raised to the use of a typewriter, provided that each typed sheet is irremovably affixed to the Minute book and initialled by the **Secretary** before being submitted for confirmation by the Lodge...

Lodge Trustees

...The Board considers that where a Lodge has property (real or otherwise), or Funds, held in Trust, it is the duty of the **Secretary** of the Lodge to keep a list of the names and addresses of the Trustees and check periodically that he is aware of their situation...

Summonses, Electronic Communication of

...the Grand Lodge approved a recommendation...that ... where the **Secretary** of a Lodge was able and willing to despatch summonses by email, ...it should be sufficient compliance … if summonses were sent by email to those members who had requested it. It was stipulated that any such request should be made in writing and on an annual basis.

The Board has given further consideration to the matter, having regard to the ever increasing use of email as a means of communication, and now recommends that a written request once made need not be renewed annually but should continue in force until further notice to the **Secretary** of the Lodge…

Registration Forms

What is the correct time for reading registration forms?

Immediately before the Ballot is taken (see Rule 164) They must be handed to the **Secretary** before proposition is made (see Rules 159, 163, and 164).

2.2.3 Lodge By-Laws

"*Every Lodge has the power of framing proper by-laws for its government…* (*Book of Constitutions* Rule 136).

In the normal course of events, Lodge by-laws are only changed or reviewed when it is perceived that the need arises, such as a moved venue or meeting date.

However, when a reprint of the by-laws is needed, many Secretaries take the opportunity to review the by-laws and to see if there is a clause that needs updating.

The by-laws themselves will set out the rules for making alterations. A model set of by-laws is issued by the Grand Secretary on behalf of the Grand Master and a set can be obtained from the Metropolitan, Provincial or District Grand Secretary.

Any new or amended set of by-laws cannot be issued or enacted until they have the approval of the Grand Master or the appropriate Metropolitan, Provincial or District Grand Master.

The Secretary should thoroughly read his own Lodge by-laws to make himself aware of any Clauses that particularly apply to his duties and to the duties of other Lodge Officers or Members.

The Clauses that particularly refer to the Secretary are likely to be similar to the following model by-laws :-

Lodge Committee

The Lodge Committee shall consist of the Master, Wardens, Past Masters of [and in] the Lodge, Treasurer, **Secretary** and other members to be elected...

Fees and Annual Subscription

The **Secretary's** services shall be deemed equivalent to payment of subscription

While Rule 104(c), *Book of Constitutions*, allows for the **Secretary's** services to be equivalent to payment of subscriptions, this is an option for the Lodge to adopt as is the provision for the Master's privilege to invite guests at the Lodge's expense.

Objections to Candidates for Initiation or Joining

If there be any objection to the introduction of a Candidate for Initiation, or a Brother for Joining, it is recommended that such objection be mentioned privately to the Master or **Secretary** who may communicate with the proposer and give him the opportunity of withdrawing his Candidate.

As can be seen from all of the above, the Secretary is bound by clear sets of Rules for significant parts of his work. The '**Defined Duties**' section is included because it is important that the Secretary knows what he is obliged to do within the Rules set down by Grand Lodge and his own Lodge by-laws.

2.3 Undefined Qualities and Responsibilities

For those who have not yet enjoyed the privilege of taking on the office, the Secretary is perceived as the person in the Lodge who is responsible for sending out the summons, preparing and reading the minutes and reading out the correspondence at the risings – oh yes and he gets his subscription for free! Well - to paraphrase Milton Friedman "There is no such thing as a free subscription!"

The Lodge Secretary has a duty to use his best endeavours to meet the obligations of his Office. He is responsible to the Master and to the Lodge for fulfilling the role in accordance with the foregoing Rules, Points of Procedure and by-laws. To do this he must apply a wide range of skills, judgement and other personal attributes.

These skills must include:-

2.3.1 Awareness of Documents and Work

The Lodge Secretary is to make himself aware of the following books, documents and information and how and when each rule, note or reference impacts on the various aspects of his role:-

- *Book of Constitutions* Rules with Updates
- *Information for the Guidance of Members of the Craft*
- Lodge by-laws
- Minute book
- Metropolitan/Provincial/District Year Book
- Masonic Year Book
- Various booklets issued by Grand Lodge
- Other reference books and papers
- Lodge programme of work
- Minutes of recent Lodge Committees
- Recent correspondence
- Any outstanding issues with Officers or Members

2.3.2 Communicate with Master and Officers

He should ascertain from other Officers, those issues under their control that impact on either what he does or how he does it, including:-

- the Master regarding Officers, Programme, Summons and Agenda items and Ceremonies.
- the Director of Ceremonies to confirm all Officers will be present or substituted and briefed.
- the Treasurer to keep abreast of Lodge Finances and members' actions and intentions particularly with regard to timely payment of subscriptions and clearance certificates
- the Almoner and Charity Steward regarding the well-being and contact details of Lodge members.
- other Lodge Officers to keep abreast of members' actions and intentions.

2.3.3 Process Forms

The Secretary must deal with all Forms from or required by Grand Lodge and Metropolitan, Provincial or District Grand Lodge including making sure they are completed properly, signed where and when necessary and submitted in time, with appropriate fees where required. These forms include:-

- Annual Returns
- Installation Returns
- Candidate/Joining Member Registration Forms
- Request for Grand Lodge Certificate
- Promotion to Metropolitan/Provincial/District Rank.
- Requests for Dispensations
- Clearance Certificates

2.3.4 Preparation

The Secretary must carry out all the necessary preparation between meetings to ensure their smooth running.

- Regular meetings
- Election meeting
- Installation meeting
- Emergency meetings
- Lodge Committee meetings

2.3.5 Action Required

The Secretary has to produce the following to pre-determined deadlines:

- Meeting agendas
- Summonses
- Meeting minutes

He also has to deal expeditiously with correspondence from Grand Lodge; Metropolitan, Provincial or District Grand Lodge; the Master, Officers and Brethren of the Lodge; other Lodges and Masons; Widows and Dependants of Past Members; service providers, suppliers and the general public.

2.3.6 Distribute

The Secretary must distribute the following to the membership, and others, by post or email including finding out number of attendees, diners and missing Officers:-

- Summons and attachments to Lodge Members
- Summons to Grand Lodge; Metropolitan, Provincial or District Grand Lodge; Visiting Officer; Visitors; Venue Managers and Caterers.
- Agenda and attachments for Lodge Committee, to Committee Members.

Electronic Communication of Formal Documents
Grand Lodge has ruled that "*…except in the case of Lodge summonses … whenever a Rule in the Book of Constitutions requires a written notice, request or document to be given by or to a specific individual or individuals that document must have been received in paper form and bear an original signature in order to be effective and to be acted upon. Accordingly a notice under Rule 106, a request under Rule 173, or a certificate under Rule 175, may not be sent by email. These are, however, examples only and are not intended to restrict the general principle stated above.*"

2.3.7 To Read and Report at Lodge Meetings
The Secretary must prepare and read to the Lodge the following documents and correspondence:-

- Lodge Minutes
- Dispensations, Propositions and Declarations
- Details of Candidates for Initiation or Joining
- Antient Charges to Master Elect
- To report the proceedings of Grand Lodge
- To report on matters concerning Metropolitan, Provincial or District Grand Lodge
- To report on Group matters
- To give notice of propositions for membership and joining
- To report apologies for absence and all other matters affecting the Lodge.

The above lists are indicative of the work involved in fulfilling the role of Lodge Secretary. Other issues will no doubt arise that need to be dealt with.

Whole sections of the work may be delegated to others to manage e.g. to a Steward responsible for managing the dining or to an Assistant Secretary who may take and distribute the minutes for the Lodge Committee.

Further details of many of these and other activities are contained in other Chapters of this book.

2.3.8 Management
The Master is in control of his Lodge and his role may be considered to be one of Chairman or Chief Executive. It is the duty and role of the Secretary to manage the Lodge affairs and ensure that all matters relating to the smooth running of the Lodge are dealt with and, where appropriate, brought to the attention of the Master, relevant officers, the Permanent Committee and/or the members.

The Secretary is also responsible for administering meetings, compiling the agenda and ensuring the designated officers and members are aware of what is required of them at each meeting relating to Agenda items.

2.3.9 Co-ordination and Liaison

The Secretary has to liaise with the Master, the Lodge executive, members and candidates.

The Secretary has to co-ordinate their activities to ensure that the appropriate representation is effected at informal meetings, candidate interviews, GP/Permanent Committee meetings, Metropolitan, Provincial or District meetings or training sessions and Grand Lodge Quarterly Communications.

He has to liaise and communicate with the Secretaries of other Lodges and co-ordinate exchange visits and/or joint activities.

He has to liaise and communicate with third party organisations arranging meeting rooms, dining, printing and other services.

2.3.10 Practical Application

The Secretary also has to be practical by producing the Summons and Minutes; completing forms for applications, promotions, annual and installation returns; dealing with correspondence; assisting with preparations for anniversaries and Centenaries.

2.3.11 Custodian

The Secretary is the custodian of Lodge records, stationery and other active property; Lodge archives and history. He has to ensure the security and confidentiality of both personal and Masonic information relating to each Lodge Member.

2.3.12 Advice and Counsel

The Secretary is called upon for advice and counsel in respect of the *Book of Constitutions* and all other matters Masonic by the Master and other Lodge members. At times, he is also contacted by members' families, candidates and other non-masons seeking information and advice.

2.3.13 Personal Attributes

In summary, to fulfil his role the Secretary should preferably have the following personal attributes:-

- He must be motivated to act on his own initiative. The role of Secretary is not one of sitting down waiting for others to do the work.
- He must be a good communicator.
- He must have discretion and perception in dealing with the confidential, personal and/or private issues relating to the Lodge, its members and their families.
- He must be dedicated to serving the Master, the Lodge and its Members and employ firm but balanced judgement and diplomacy in the application of the rules and in the execution of his other duties.

CHAPTER 3

ACCEPTING THE POSITION OF LODGE SECRETARY

3.1 Generally

To be offered the position of Lodge Secretary is an honour carrying with it many responsibilities. It is a position that should neither be offered nor taken on lightly.

In larger lodges there are often a number of members who would be suitable for the role and several who would be willing to accept it. In the smaller or 'shrinking' Lodges, finding a suitable member to accept the role is often more difficult.

Once a Secretary is in office, he tends to be there for some years, as is appropriate for continuity and stability. It is suggested that a minimum of three years should be considered as being the time required to learn the role, become competent and to enjoy it. Secretaries often become very protective of the role and are happy to continue in office for many years. Serving over ten years as Secretary or in any other non-progressive office is frowned upon by Grand Lodge.

3.2 The Learning Curve

The factors that have a significant impact on the length of the learning curve for each new Secretary are:-

3.2.1 The Competency and Effectiveness of The outgoing Secretary

It will always be easier to take over from a Secretary who has administered the Lodge in a proper and efficient manner, has kept tidy records of meetings and correspondence and has recorded all past, ongoing and proposed activities and events.

If the information is properly recorded, either manually or electronically in a bespoke program, database or spreadsheet, then continuity and taking over as Secretary become more straightforward.

3.2.2 Quality and Format of Handover Information

Most new Secretaries receive Lodge information from their predecessor in a number of boxes, some of which contain historical information and some of the boxes may not have been opened by one or more of his predecessors.

Each past Secretary will have had idiosyncrasies relating to his filing methods. These will range from just putting everything into a box marked "Lodge 2009" through to providing different files for each category, sorted by date and with file notes for cross-referencing where helpful.

Unsubmitted Annual or Installation Returns and other forms, inconsistencies in member data and 'apparently' missing documents are indications that your early workload as Secretary may be heavier that you anticipated.

The advent of computers can make tracking correspondence more difficult rather than easier if not properly managed, particularly if no printed copy has been made of an incoming or outgoing letter or email.

The location and nomenclature of a computer based file or email may be very difficult to find.

3.2.3 Lodge Custom and Expectations

The method of operation of your predecessor and his predecessors and the expectations of various Past Masters and senior Masons will no doubt be communicated to you with advice that you should 'follow' or 'change' previous practice.

The content, correctness, appearance and quality of the Lodge Summons is always an area that receives particular attention.

Ultimately it is the Secretary who has to produce all documents and administer the Lodge and its members. It would be prudent to assess what has to be delivered and how it is best achieved to meet the requirements of the Lodge, the *Book of Constitutions* and yourself.

If you wish to make changes that will affect the membership (e.g. circulate minutes rather than read them or email the summons rather than post it), discuss your ideas with the Master and take your proposal to the Lodge Committee.

3.3 Commitment

There cannot be many brethren who accept the position of Lodge Secretary without realising that they are committing themselves to fulfilling a role that takes time and involves significant effort.

3.3.1 Time Commitment

There are tangible time commitments associated with the role of Secretary that fall into three categories:-

- An initial period of becoming acquainted with the role, the history of the Lodge, member and meeting details and (perhaps) conversion of some or all paper based information to computer based records.
- Ongoing regular activities that are directly influenced by the number of members and the frequency of meetings.
- Event based activities such as new or leaving members, promotions, training seminars, Lodge Anniversaries, Grand Lodge and Provincial Returns, Lodge Committee Meetings, by-law changes and dealing with correspondence.

3.3.2 Deadlines To Be Met

The Secretary's role is much concerned with the meeting of deadlines and therefore requires good time management and discipline:-

The key deadlines that have to be met are:-

- Preparation, printing and distribution of Summons.
- Preparation (and distribution) of Meeting Minutes.
- Initiation of and response to correspondence.
- Requests and payment for dispensations.
- Request for and issue of Certificates.
- Completion and submission of forms for Promotions, Installation and Annual Returns.
- Ascertainment of festive board dining numbers and requirements and placing of orders.

CHAPTER 4

THE TRANSFER OF LODGE PROPERTY, DOCUMENTS AND INFORMATION

4.1 Generally

The ownership of all Lodge Property is transferred every year into the hands of the new Master and Wardens unless it is held by special trustees. The physical movement of the paperwork associated with the history and management of a Lodge takes place every five years or so when a new Secretary takes Office.

The *Book of Constitutions* states in Rule 143

> *"All property of a Lodge not vested in special trustees belongs to, and is the property of, the Master and Wardens for the time being, in trust for the members of the Lodge. If any Lodge shall pledge its jewels and furniture or any part thereof, or permit or suffer any charge or lien thereon to arise or to be created, then its warrant is liable to be forfeited. Every member of a Lodge is bound on ceasing to hold an office in the Lodge forthwith to hand over to his successor in such office all books, papers, documents, and other property, if any, in his possession or under his control by virtue of his having held such office."*

Information for the Guidance of Members of the Craft states:-

> *"Lodges are advised to take steps for the permanent housing of Lodge records which have ceased to be of day-to-day use. The Board suggests that in order to ensure that future Office holders or historians are aware of where the records have been deposited (e.g. the Lodge's Bankers), a comprehensive list be placed in the current Minute book and transferred to its successor when its turn comes to be laid up in safe-keeping."*

The Secretary, by his Office, is charged to hold and/or keep records of the Lodge Property, Documents and Information.

4.2 Recording of Documents Transferred

The physical transfer of information from one Secretary to his successor generally requires the exchange of a number of boxes of documents, certificates, books, jewels, collars and other information and property.

This information often comprises all or part of the Lodge History as well as the current management files. As such, the new Secretary will be required to provide or arrange safe and secure storage space.

At the most simple level, the handover should include an inventory of all that is being handed over with numbered and catalogued boxes.

If this has not been done already, it is suggested that the new Secretary prepares an inventory and sends the list to his predecessor, for agreement and for avoidance of future problems should some property, documents or boxes disappear.

The inventory should include reference to any archived documents, their location (if not handed over) and the name and address of the member responsible for them. Should such a member either leave or pass to Grand Lodge above, arrangements should be made to collect and re-store.

Handed over documents and property can include the following:-

- Active Lodge information and electronic data
- Books and other Lodge property
- Archived Lodge information

4.3 Active Lodge Information and Electronic Data

The nature of active Lodge information has not changed for centuries – summons, minutes and correspondence.

However over the past three decades the advent of computers and electronic data storage has brought significant changes in the forms of communication and the ways that information is prepared, despatched, filed and stored. The impact of these changes is addressed more fully later in Chapter 12.

The following list of 'Active' Lodge documents constitutes the papers that the new Secretary has to study when he first takes office in order to provide continuity, meet deadlines and arrive at Lodge meetings with the right tools and information.

4.3.1 THE ACTIVE LODGE DOCUMENTS INCLUDE:

- **Open Correspondence** - Correspondence can be considered as open if it is yet to be answered or is part of an ongoing string of correspondence.

  It is useful for the Secretary to read past correspondence to appreciate how his predecessor and Lodge members dealt with and reacted to events. It is his responsibility to pick up the threads and continue to deal with ongoing issues.

  The use of emails that are received by and sent from the personal mailbox of previous Secretaries can be a problem. It is quite possible that neither the incoming email nor the reply are printed or saved into any Lodge record. This issue is discussed further in 4.3.2 below.
- **Recent relevant Summonses.** Copies of old Summonses are to be archived but more recent ones can be used as a template or as an aide memoire for similar meetings.
- **Current Minute Book.** The minute book(s) provides the base information for the incoming Secretary to confirm or build up his knowledge of arrivals and departures; past and current offices held by members; promotions; and correspondence and edicts from Grand Lodge and other Masonic authorities.
- **Current Attendance Book.** This is needed as reference for recording attendance in the minutes. It is also useful in assessing the commitment of members for Lodge Office and the attendance record of past masters when recommendations for promotion are being considered.
- **Grand Lodge Forms** – It is probable that the incoming Secretary will have to complete the Installation Return immediately upon being appointed into office. It is likely that forms for initiates and joining members are in need of attention. In addition, a supply of blank forms should always be available to pass to members who have candidates.
- **Dispensations and Certificates.** There are well over a dozen reasons that the Secretary is required to issue or request a Certificate or seek a Dispensation relating to members, meetings and ceremonies. The Secretary must be aware of the need to take timely and appropriate action in this regard. (See Chapter 9.1.2)
- **Supplier Details.** The Secretary will immediately have to enter into dialogue with and meet the requirements, prices and deadlines of service suppliers. This will include ensuring that menus and dining numbers are provided to the caterer and draft summons to the printer.

4.3.2 Handover of Multimedia Data

Generally

In 1981, the IBM PC was launched and personal computers as we have known them have been in use since then. It is probable that at least some of the information that is handed over to the new Secretary will be in electronic format. There are likely to be issues surrounding this information (data) caused by computers, software and the way that data has been handled. This section considers those matters related to the handover of computer generated data and the problems that may be encountered.

The information is likely to be data base or spreadsheet files or word processing documents or a combination of all three. The format of the information will vary depending on its age and the software used to prepare, process and save it.

The information will probably include parts of the Lodge history. It may be saved on different forms of storage media that could include obsolete magnetic media including 8", 5¼" or 3½" floppy disks, a range of magnetic tape back-up formats through to CDs, DVDs or Memory Sticks.

Difficulty in accessing the data can be for the following reasons:-

Hardware problems

Hardware includes computers, disk drives and disks, tape back-up systems and magnetic tapes, memory sticks and other back-up systems. Hardware issues include:-

- outdated storage media may have been used to store data
- the disk drives or tape readers to open the storage media are no longer available
- the storage media has become damaged or deteriorated.

Software problems

Software will include the programs used or needed to open the files to access the data; and the format and type of file on which the data had been saved. Software issues include:-

- outdated versions of software may have been used to generate or save data.
- newer versions of software may have been used to generate or save data.
- the software program necessary to read and open the data files is no longer available.

- the files or the program to open the files may have become corrupted or infected with a virus.

All of these hardware and software issues mean that there may be problems in opening and viewing information for 'mechanical reasons'.

User problems

The manner in which the data has been saved, recorded and/or password protected creates the next potential problem. Many of the problems with computers relate to the people who use them. This can be due to:-

- different users doing things in different ways.
- users being uncertain of what they are doing, but doing it anyway.
- names of older files being only 8 characters long or fewer.
- files not saved in a structured directory.
- if the 'computer clock' was not set, the date the file was created or saved will not be known.
- the data file may be corrupted or password protected.

If all or most of the above apply, it may mean that you do not know what the file is, to what it alludes or when it was saved – and it may not be possible to open it.

The above examples are real and are likely to apply in most Lodges to a greater or lesser extent. As a consequence, some Lodge history may be lost forever.

Therefore a comprehensive inventory gains more importance as the further one moves from a set of lost or inaccessible information, the less likely that anything can be done to recover it.

Action to resolve hardware and software problems

To avoid future problems, paper copies should be taken of all important documents including emails, in and out. In addition, occasional print-outs of membership and Lodge data bases should be taken and kept safely.

It should be remembered that not all computer files are critical and there may be printed copies of the minutes, correspondence, summons or reports on the Lodge files.

Before becoming too concerned or taking drastic action, it is essential to determine what Lodge information is held and what critical data may be missing, if any. Data/information may be considered critical if it is required to prove that the Lodge has an uninterrupted history or relates to a subject that has been passed to Grand Lodge for disciplinary action or appeal.

If you have complete sets of Lodge information and history, then it should be recorded as such.

If the Lodge information is not complete, identify exactly when and where the voids occur, who was Secretary at the time and where the missing information data was held and if it may be recovered.

Find out from your predecessor(s) if he or they still have the means of reading the storage media so that you can at least list the files. (They may have duplicates of the data stored in more accessible media or format).

- If the files can be read, they should be copied into a readable format onto a currently accessible type of media. Print out relevant files and place in the Lodge records.
- If they cannot be read, endeavour to determine how old the files are and whether they contain critical information. (See 'Sources of Help and Advice' below).

Action to resolve user problems

If the files are in a mess there is little that can be done other than to create a set of directories appropriate to your Lodge, open each file in turn, rename it if necessary and save it in the relevant directory.

If files are locked with a password or will not open, refer to your predecessor.

Sources of help and advice

Always look first to the person who you think generated or accessed the data last – i.e. your predecessors.

- Enquire if there is anyone in Lodge who is particularly computer literate and may be able to help. He may assist in setting up a structured directory in which to save Lodge files.
- Search the Internet with Google or other search engine, briefly stating your question (five or six words) and try and find a helpful response. You will be surprised at how many times your problem is answered.
- Go to the hardware or software manufacturer's page on the internet stating your question in detail on their 'Help' page and try and find a helpful response. You will usually be first referred to the FAQ page.
- Ask your Metropolitan, Provincial or District Grand Secretary. He is likely to have been asked similar questions on other occasions and may know someone who can help.

- Ask the UK Mason List which is a Masonic Internet Forum. There are some very computer-literate subscribers who may be able to assist with more difficult technical problems.

Unrecorded emails

The general advice given above is applicable in most circumstances but the issue of correspondence exchanged by email, but not saved in the Lodge records, is given a special mention as it is likely to be a more recent phenomenon and may be more easily recoverable than some of the older issues.

Unrecorded emails occur when emails to or from a Lodge Secretary are not scheduled, no print-out has been taken and no copy of the email passed across with the Lodge Documents.

When the current correspondence has been studied and any obvious voids or references to emails are picked up, efforts should be made immediately to recover any unrecorded email in case they are deleted.

The following steps may be taken to mitigate the chances of such data being permanently lost or destroyed:-

Immediately upon receiving the Lodge information from your predecessor, ask if there are any emails received or sent and whether the copies are on the disk/CD/memory stick that has been handed over. Some answers could be:

a) "Yes – everything is there." - Ask where the emails are stored, what issues were dealt with by email and whether there are any outstanding issues not yet dealt with.
b) "No, I don't use email and I don't know about my predecessors." Depending how long your predecessor had been in post, any problems you have may not relate to computer data. If he was only in post for a short time carry out the checks for voids in information, possibly applicable to his predecessors.
c) "I don't think so." Ask your predecessor to use the email search engine to look through his past correspondence for the Lodge Name, the Lodge Number and other likely words such as the Master's name, 'candidate', 'dues', 'exclusion', and 'member' to find any relevant incoming or outgoing emails.
d) "I am not sure but I've deleted all my old emails anyway." Enquire if there are any outstanding issues and whether they were being dealt with by email. If there are issues outstanding, ask the third party involved to copy all past emails to you as you are now Secretary.
e) Oh! I forgot about the emails. As c) above.

Ultimately, you can only deal with what you have. Important issues should be recorded in the minutes of Lodge and Lodge Committee meetings, and Lodge data recorded in Installation and Annual Returns. However lost emails regarding resignations or notifications of country membership can be difficult when differences arise related to subscriptions. This has now been addressed by the *Information for the Guidance of Members of the Craft* - Electronic Communication of Formal Documents (See Chapters 2.2.6 and 8.2.1)

On the positive side, electronic information properly researched, saved and managed can mean that all the data on members and meetings will be structured, members' progress, status and relevant details will be instantly available and the production of reports, letters and labels can be available at the 'touch of a button'.

It also means that communication with Members, other Lodges, Grand Lodge, Metropolitan, Provincial or District Grand Lodges and service providers can be carried out in the most efficient and cost-effective manner.

4.4 Books and Other Lodge Property

With 75% of Lodges in the UK being over 50 years old and nearly 300 Lodges over 200 years old, the quantity and bulk of property that is held can be significant and will include:-

4.4.1 Books – Active Books

Book of Constitutions - The Secretary is required to have a number of copies of the *Book of Constitutions*, kept up to date with all issued revisions.

The *Book of Constitutions* is the Secretary's first point of reference when issues arise in the Lodge and his own copy will no doubt become as well thumbed as an old ritual book.

As well as for his own use, copies of the *Book of Constitutions* need to be kept for issue to each Candidate, Joining Member from a different Constitution and each new Master.

The latest version of *Information for the Guidance of Members of the Craft* is issued to accompany the *Book of Constitutions* and is to be read in conjunction with it.

The Booklet entitled *The Masonic Charities* is also packaged with the *Book of Constitutions.*

The Secretary should ensure that his Lodge By-laws are up to date and that sufficient copies exist.

Commemorative Booklets. Many Lodges record their Lodge History and commemorate Centenaries or other significant dates by the publication of a

Booklet. Copies of these booklets are often given to New Candidates at their initiation. The Secretary should check whether reprints of these booklets are necessary. When one is produced it is good practice to deposit a copy with the Library at Freemasons' Hall.

4.4.2 Books – Reference Books

There are many books published that may be used for reference by the Secretary.

Masonic Year Books and Directories. These record details and contact information of Grand Lodge or Metropolitan, Provincial or District Grand Lodges and Private Lodges, meeting places, dates and Officers. They are issued annually to each Secretary by Grand Lodge and the relevant Province.

Guidance Notes for Secretaries have often been produced and issues by the Metropolitan, Provincial or District Grand Lodges. Additional copies are usually available either free or at a modest price.

Research Papers and Other Books – Many Lodges subscribe to Quatuor Coronati and other Masonic Research lodges who publish research papers and lectures.

The existence of these should be made known to members in order that they may extend their Masonic Knowledge as part of their "...daily advancement...".

Various tomes and books, either acquired by past Secretaries or donated by members and past members, are often passed to the Secretary with other Lodge Property. The existence of these should also be made known to brethren for Masonic Research or extending their Masonic Knowledge.

4.4.3 Other Lodge Property

There may be other items of Lodge Property that are physically handed to the Secretary or for which he becomes wholly or partially responsible. Whether these come under his charge or not, he should be aware of their existence together with the contact name and address of any Custodian or Trustee. Where appropriate, the Secretary should make himself aware of any terms of reference and/or document expiry dates pertaining to Lodge property, agreements or insurances.

Buildings and Title Deeds. It is likely that a Board of Trustees will manage any building property owned by the Lodge with appropriate documents safely lodged with a Bank. Leases, Tenancies and Rent Agreements may be managed by Lawyers, Accountants, Surveyors or Trustees. It will be the Secretary's responsibility to incorporate any required reports from such Groups into the Lodge Committee Meeting agendas.

Many Lodges own **Bonds, Shares and other Investments**. Whilst the Treasurer would normally be responsible to account for them, the Secretary should be aware of their existence and have details of who is responsible for their custody and management.

Furniture, Pictures, Regalia, Banners, Jewels and other valuables should be catalogued, their condition recorded and insured. It would be prudent to photograph unique or valuable items in the event of theft or damage.

The Lodge Box. The 'Lodge Box' is usually kept at the Lodge Meeting place and contains Lodge Room furnishings, officers' regalia, declaration books, attendance books, aprons etc. Its contents are often only seen by the Tyler who prepares the Lodge Room in advance of meetings.

The replacement cost of contents of the Lodge Box could easily be in excess of £5,000 so insurance against theft, damage or fire may be considered prudent, unless the Lodge Meeting place provides cover. This matter should be dealt with by the Secretary and the Lodge Committee.

The Secretary should liaise with the Tyler to get an up-to-date inventory of the box and a note of the condition of its contents.

The Lodge Computer - An increasing number of Lodges are purchasing a computer and/or software to assist in the management of the Lodge affairs. These should be insured, regularly backed-up and with back-ups retained by another Lodge Officer (perhaps the Treasurer).

He should also ensure that all correspondence and other information managed on a computer is properly catalogued, stored and backed-up, with back-ups passed to the Treasurer or other Lodge officer for safe keeping on a regular basis. Where appropriate, emails should be transferred to a recoverable saved document. Hard copies should be taken of all important documents.

It would be prudent to develop the routine of exchanging data back-ups with the Treasurer at every meeting (including correspondence, member details, summonses, emails, accounts, orders, invoices and program data back-up).

It follows that the Secretary should maintain and care for all the information and property that he holds and keeps the inventory up to date so that when it comes to transferring to his successor, or in the event of his untimely demise, everything is in good order.

CHAPTER 5
GRAND LODGE, METROPOLITAN, PROVINCIAL & DISTRICT GRAND LODGE

5.1 The Grand Lodge

5.1.1 Generally

The Lodge Secretary will have little involvement with the Grand Lodge. With very few exceptions all communications of the Lodge Secretary will be through the Metropolitan, Provincial or District Grand Lodge.

Correspondence from Grand Lodge will include receipt by the Secretary of the Quarterly Communications and Summons; Grand Charity Annual Reports; Notices of Grand Lodge Dues and Room Charges; updates to the *Book of Constitutions* and *Information for Guidance of the Members of the Craft*; Masonic Year Book and various other letters containing Grand Lodge News.

The Lodge Secretary should not need to write to the Grand Secretary regarding any matters unless Grand Secretary has specifically written to him and asked for a response.

All matters should as matter of course be channelled through the Metropolitan, Provincial or District Grand Lodge including requests for Dispensations that are issued by Grand Master, Installation Returns and Annual Returns, promotions to Grand Rank and questions regarding the interpretation of Grand Lodge documents.

If there is an issue of any sort that needs elevating to Grand Lodge, it must be done via the Metropolitan, Provincial or District Grand Secretary.

5.1.2 Publications

Book of Constitutions

The main publication from Grand Lodge is the Book of Constitutions, the rules of which govern Freemasonry in all of its Lodges. It is updated by circulated Addenda as issued from the Board of General Purposes with consolidated new editions when needed, usually between 2 and 3 years.

The *Book of Constitutions* is presented to every Candidate at his Initiation, every Master at his Installation and every Joining Member from a different Constitution when becoming a member of a Lodge.

Information for the Guidance of Members of the Craft

Information for the Guidance of Members of the Craft does what it says on the cover. It is produced by The Board of General Purposes of Grand Lodge and is a compilation of practical matters and clarification and interpretation of Rules from the Book of Constitution. It is updated annually.

The Booklet is packaged with the *Book of Constitutions* and is available separately from Grand Lodge.

Masonic Yearbook and Directory of Lodges and Chapters

The Masonic Yearbook is published every year and is despatched free of charge to each Secretary.

Directory of Lodges and Chapters is published every three years and is despatched free of charge to each Secretary.

Masonic Information Pack

Grand Lodge also publishes a Candidates Pack that includes seven small booklets. Together they are a most attractive set, very informative and a great help to pass to anyone who is seriously considering applying to become a Freemason:

Two white ones entitled:-

- Freemasonry: An Approach to Life
- Your Questions Answered

and a package of five fold-out brochures entitled:

- What is Freemasonry
- Freemasonry and Society
- Freemasonry and Religion
- Regular Freemasonry and Public Affairs
- Freemasonry's External Relations

5.1.3 Technology

Grand Lodge Computer Data Base

The Grand Lodge has a database management system called "ADelphi" looking after all Member details. Over the past five years, it has been deployed to many Provinces who now use it as their Member management system, some exclusively and some in conjunction with their other legacy software.

Those Provinces who use it exclusively will employ the Grand Lodge Computer Reference as the unique identifier for each Mason which will ultimately regularise the total Member data base. This number appears against each Member's name on the Annual Returns, issued by Grand Lodge.

Grand Lodge Website (www.ugle.org.uk)

The Grand Lodge Website that was updated in September 2009 gives access to an electronic version (pdf or txt file) of the latest update of the *Book of Constitutions* both for the Craft and Royal Arch and of the *Information for the Guidance of Members of the Craft*, all of great use to the Lodge Secretary.

The remainder of the Website is primarily 'outward facing' and provides help and information for Masons and non-masons alike.

Electronic Forms

The only Grand Lodge Form that is currently available in electronic format is the LP&A5 Application Form for a Grand Lodge Certificate. It is available in the form of a template with highlighted fields into which the details of the Lodge, the Candidate(s) and the Secretary can be entered. The Form can then be despatched to Metropolitan, Provincial or District Grand Lodge who will forward it to Grand Lodge.

It would not be a great surprise if all other Grand Lodge Forms become available in electronic format over the next few years. Rule 191C already provides for this to take place.

Provincial and Lodge Websites

Grand Lodge have published a paper "*Guidance for Members of the Craft and Royal Arch on the use of the Internet and World Wide Web for communicating and informing*". It includes a clearly defined policy to prevent breach of Rule 177 – Printing or Publishing Proceedings.

The paper includes "Suggested content of a Lodge or Chapter Web Site" and "Password protected area".

It stresses that no personal names, details or photos can be included without the written permission of **all** individuals concerned.

It also states that there should be no advertising or commercial links and specifically directs that no mention or links to the Website designer should be included.

Lodges should submit the proposed content of any Websites for approval by the Grand Secretary before they are published on the World Wide Web. If approved, the website will be authorised to carry the Grand Lodge charter mark.

Electronic Communication of Formal Documents

Grand Lodge has ruled that "…except in the case of Lodge summonses …whenever a Rule in the *Book of Constitutions* requires a written notice, request or document to be given by or to a specific individual or individuals that document must have been received in paper form and bear an original signature in order to be effective and to be acted upon." This is covered further in Chapters 2.2.6 and 8.2.2.

5.1.4 Other Relevant Administrative Issues

Mentoring

In December 2007, UGLE published its "Rulers Forum - Working Party Report on Mentoring", a 194 page document. The report addressed in depth all the issues of caring for its new members, communicating understanding and knowledge and encouraging active involvement without pressurising, and avoiding premature attachment to other orders.

There are many ways of approaching Mentoring. With the benefit of the report, Metropolitan, Provincial or District Grand Lodges were encouraged to consider the subject and many have implemented their own systems.

Promotions

Every Grand Officer is appointed by the Grand Master. Almost without exception, appointments to Grand Office will be based on recommendations from or passed through Metropolitan, Provincial or District Grand Masters.

Visiting Officers and Official Visits

Visiting Officers are all organised through Metropolitan, Provincial or District Grand Lodge.

All official visits are organised through Metropolitan, Provincial or District Grand Lodge. If a Lodge is holding its Bi-Centenary or 250th Anniversary, it is probable that Grand Lodge will be formally represented. However, all the arrangements will be made and agreed through Province.

Grand Lodge Forms

All Grand Lodge Forms including Registration Forms, Annual Return and Installation Returns must be sent to Grand Lodge with the appropriate Fees, when requested. In most instances they should be returned to the Metropolitan,

Provincial or District Grand Secretary who will forward them to Grand Lodge. It is important to follow the instructions given by the Metropolitan, Provincial or District Grand Secretary in this regard.

Grand Lodge Fees

The adjustment of Grand Lodge Fees is agreed at the Grand Lodge Meeting in June. Detailed notices are sent out via the Lodge Secretary in September and again December. The Secretary must ensure that he passes the information to the Lodge Treasurer.

All increases come into effect on 1st January.

All Fees are chargeable based on the rates chargeable at the date they are received by Grand Lodge rather than the date of the Ceremony/Registration or the date due. It is therefore to the advantage of the Lodge to submit Forms with Fees as soon as possible, especially around the turn of the year.

Dispensations

The issue of most Dispensations has been delegated to Metropolitan, Provincial or District Grand Masters.

The exceptions to this are as follows:-

Rule 90 Conferment of degrees at short intervals (Lodges Abroad). Dispensation has to be obtained from Grand Master or District Grand Master.

Rule 115 No Brother shall be Master of two or more Lodges at the same time. Dispensation has to be obtained from Grand Master (or District Grand Master if both Lodges are in the same District).

Rule 172 Degree ceremonies less than 28 days apart (No Dispensation is available in advance but the Grand Master may issue a retrospective Dispensation, otherwise the ceremony is void).

Rule 188 Lodge with less than five members. Dispensation has to be obtained from Grand Master.

District Grand Masters have delegated authority to grant Dispensations for Rules 90 and 115 due to issues of distance.

In every case, the Dispensation should be applied for through the Metropolitan, Provincial or District Grand Lodge.

5.2 Metropolitan, Provincial and District Grand Lodge

5.2.1 Generally

The responsibility for co-ordinating and administering Private Lodges has been delegated to the Metropolitan, Provincial and District Grand Lodges by the Grand Lodge.

Each Metropolitan, Provincial and District Grand Lodge acts largely as an autonomous unit.

5.2.2 Communication

The Lodge Secretary's position vis à vis the Metropolitan, Provincial or District Grand Lodge is that he is the first point of contact between the Executive and the Lodge.

Unless the Secretary is contacted directly by Grand Lodge and asked to respond, there is scarcely an occasion that the Lodge Secretary needs to make direct contact with Grand Lodge.

Newsletters

Most Metropolitan, Provincial and District Grand Lodges produce Newsletters that provide news of Provincial appointments, and reports and pictures of Provincial, Lodge, Charity and Social events. The frequency of the Newsletters varies from Province to Province.

Notifications

Although Grand Lodge has permitted certain documents to be transmitted by email, this does not apply to formal notifications. A reference in *Information for the Guidance for Members of the Craft* states that "*... a notice under Rule 106, a request under Rule 173, or a certificate under Rule 175, may not be sent by email.*" See also Section 2.3.6 above (Page 27).

If the Secretary is in doubt as to whether an email request for a Dispensation is sufficient, he should check with his Metropolitan, Provincial or District Grand Secretary.

Send documents in good time

The Metropolitan, Provincial or District Grand Lodge is responsible for the administration of all Grand Lodge documents and issues, as well as its own.

Therefore it is beholden upon the Lodge Secretary to ensure that all Forms, Returns and Notifications are sent to the Metropolitan, Provincial or District Grand Secretary, promptly, properly completed and checked, accompanied by the correct Fees where appropriate.

The activities of the Visiting Officers vary from Province to Province. Where the Visiting Officer completes a Return for the Lodges of which he is responsible, the Lodge Secretary is often asked to assist in this task by completing details such as number of attendees and diners.

Provincial Website

Most Metropolitan, Provincial or District Websites provide a wealth of information for Lodge Secretaries including the ability to download relevant forms, advisory Booklets like the Secretary's Handbook, standard Forms and documents such as Lodge by-laws, meeting agendas and toast lists.

However some of the above information, forms and documents are for the purposes of housekeeping and administration. By their very nature, (like the back office, the broom cupboard, the box room and the boiler house) they would not be recommended for inclusion on a website that is our 'shop window'.

It is therefore likely that many Provinces will follow the example of Metropolitan Grand Lodge and have two sites, one for General Information and one for Lodge Secretaries and others who have to assist in the administration of the Lodge.

The alternative to this is having a 'password access' section, which appears to those who are denied access as either secret or elitist and defeats the objective of openness that is created by having a Website.

The rules and standards set by Grand Lodge relating to the use and development of Websites apply equally to Provinces as they do to individual Lodges, with the same reward, the use of the Grand Lodge Charter Mark, if the Website is approved.

One of the results of this is that many of the Provincial Officers are referred to by their position rather than their name. Also details of any Lodge Members can only be accessed via links to Lodge Websites, where any names or details appearing will have received the explicit approval of the Lodge Members concerned.

The practice by some Provinces of providing email addresses for each secretary, such as sec1111@xxxshirepgl.org.uk will doubtless become more widespread.

This provides great benefits as it gives continuity of email through successive Secretaries, maintains anonymity but gives more information (the Secretary of Lodge No 1111 in the Province of Xxxshire).

It also means that emails to and from the Secretary will not get lost in the melee of personal, business or other Lodge email.

The use of email is looked at more fully in Chapter 12.1.3.

5.2.3 Promotions

Appointments and Promotions to Metropolitan, Provincial or District Honours are managed by the respective Provincial Office. Details of the Lodge Secretary's role is explained in Chapter 11.2.

All Metropolitan, Provincial or District Grand Lodges will provide a set of guidelines stating exactly what is required of the Secretary with respect to the nomination and proposition of a Lodge Member for Honours. This will be sent out to the Secretary along with the Application Form. If further information is required, the Visiting Officer or the Metropolitan, Provincial or District Grand Secretary will be pleased to assist.

The Deadline Dates for submission of Forms for each type of Appointment or Promotion will be distributed to Secretaries in good time every year and the information will usually be available of the Provincial Website and/or in the Secretaries Handbook.

The part played in the process of Members gaining Honours by the Visiting Officer should not be ignored as he is the conduit and point of contact with the Executive Office that is responsible for direct communication with your Lodge. He can give advice on ensuring that every detail that counts towards a submission being successful is included either on the Form or in the accompanying papers.

A good and open relationship with the Visiting Officer will enable the Master and the Secretary to explain the merits of the Candidate in person, which when coupled with the submission and his knowledge of the individual from Lodge visits, will enable him to communicate with the Metropolitan, Provincial or District Grand Master and his officers.

5.2.4 Official Visits

There are five levels of visits to Lodges that have to be considered and managed by Metropolitan, Provincial or District Grand Lodges.

The Lodge Secretary's involvement is described in Chapter 11.6.

The five levels of visits are:-

1 Grand Lodge Occasion
These would include Bicentenary or 250th Anniversary. The point of contact for these is the Metropolitan, Provincial or District Grand Secretary who will arrange any formal Grand Lodge presence.
2 Metropolitan, Provincial or District Grand Lodge Occasion
These would include Consecration, Centenary, Amalgamations, Banner Dedications.
3 Other Celebratory Event
These would include Long Service, all anniversaries except above, Charity Donations.
4 Official Metropolitan, Provincial or District Visit
These would include any Metropolitan, Provincial or District Grand Officer from the Deputy Metropolitan, Provincial or District Grand Master to the Visiting Officer, for the purpose of getting to know members
5 Unofficial Visits
Guests of Lodge or Members

In respect of Official Visits, the Metropolitan, Provincial or District Grand Lodge will manage and advise on all administrative arrangements including:-

- details of protocol relating to the Guest of Honour and his Escort Team,
- advise on payment for dining
- provide typical wording for Lodge Summons

5.2.5 Other Metropolitan, Provincial or District Grand Lodge Initiatives

Lodge Mentors

Grand Lodge has given the subject of Mentoring considerable thought and attention in the past five years as a result of self examination within Freemasonry and its efforts to keep new members.

There are many complex issues and differing requirements of individuals, Lodges and Provinces. Metropolitan, Provincial and District Grand Lodges have been encouraged by Grand Lodge to set up and implement systems that they feel appropriate in context with their other ongoing Membership support initiatives.

Where Mentoring systems have been adopted, they include:-

- ad hoc arranged by Lodges promoted by guidelines from Province
- Lodges having one Mentor looking after all new Masons with reports on progress and achievements kept and monitored by Provincial Offices
- Provision of Masonic log books giving candidates information at each stage from pre-initiation to Master Mason, progressively providing more information.

The Grand Lodge Report recommends that the Mentor should not hold any other demanding office (such as Secretary). This means that the Lodge Secretary's role in mentoring will depend upon how and whether a system has been taken up by the Metropolitan, Provincial or District Grand Lodge.

The Secretary will doubtless liaise with the Provincial and or Lodge Mentor (or Mentors), will include 'Mentoring' on the Agenda for each Lodge Committee meeting and, bearing in mind his one to one contact at each meeting, provide feedback and encouragement relating to the newer members.

Loss of Members

Some Provinces also have initiatives addressing the situation of when a Member resigns. These schemes endeavour to determine the reason for the resignation, and/or attempt to prevent the resignee from leaving the Craft altogether by identifying a more convenient local meeting place or a Lodge to which he may be better suited. With some schemes, the Secretary works in conjunction with the Visiting Officer and the Province.

Training

Most Metropolitan, Provincial and District Grand Lodges organise occasional Training sessions for Secretaries, Treasurers, Almoners and Charity Stewards.

These events and courses are highly recommended as they provide the following benefits;

- a point of social contact with other officers in the Province.
- an informal open forum to seek and share advice on real issues related to each office.
- brings the officers up to date with changes at Provincial and Grand Lodge.
- serves to bring an element of standardisation of reporting to Province.
- gives a level of understanding as to why, when and how information is required by Province.

It is for the Secretary to distribute the notices of the events to other Lodge Officers and to encourage attendance.

CHAPTER 6

LODGE DETAILS

6.1 Lodge Venue

The venue and dates for Lodge meetings are to be as stated in the Lodge by-laws. Specific rules and procedures apply if one wishes to change the venue, whether permanently, for one meeting or several meetings. These procedures include approvals and dispensations.

6.1.1 Permanent Changing Venue and/or Dates

The procedures necessary to deal with a Lodge that has to permanently relocate fall under Rule 141 – Removal of Lodges.

Permanent relocation can occur for a number of reasons including cost of rooms, quality or cost of dining, venue closing or for shift of membership.

As a change of meeting place can be stressful and emotive, the process should be handled with tact and consideration, particularly for members who consider themselves adversely affected by the move.

The subject of relocation will normally be debated extensively amongst the members and in the Lodge Committee. The work required of the Secretary can be summarised as follows:-

- If it is necessary to arrange an interim venue, between leaving your existing meeting place and using an unspecified future meeting place, a dispensation is needed to authorise the Lodge to meet. This can be obtained for single meetings or for a 'specified period'.
- As regards the permanent move, ensure that adequate debate has taken place.
- Give consideration to and clearly set down all options.
- Draft a Notice of Motion relating to the proposed venue change together with consequential amended meeting dates.

- The Notice of Motion should include the proposed changes to the by-laws because if the Motion is subsequently carried it is deemed to sanction associated by-laws amendments.
- The Motion must be signed by at least seven subscribing members before it can be put to the Lodge at a regular meeting (The Notice of Motion has to be presented at a Regular Meeting but the Meeting to discuss and vote on the Motion may be either a Regular Meeting or Emergency Meeting).
- So far as is possible, ensure that a two-thirds majority in favour of the proposal is likely to be achieved. If in doubt, it would be advisable to call an emergency meeting (see Chapter 6.2.3) to specifically discuss the options and decide upon the course of action, rather than risk an unsuccessful vote at a Regular Meeting.
- The Motion is to be placed on the summons for the next regular meeting (or emergency meeting). The summons is to be delivered to members not less than seven days before the meeting.
- The Motion shall only be carried if two-thirds of the members present vote in favour of it. It should be noted that an abstention counts as a 'No' vote. One should also be careful not to count non-members in the numbers of members present.

N.B. No changes can take effect until consents of the Grand Master and any affected Metropolitan, Provincial or District Grand Masters have been obtained. If moving to a different Province, two sets of consent will be required in addition to that of the Grand Master.

6.1.2 Temporary Changing of Venue

If a Lodge is required to hold an individual Lodge meeting at other than its regular venue, for whatever reason, a dispensation is required.

This must be applied for from the Grand Master, or the Metropolitan, Provincial or District Grand Master as the case may be, to meet at a specified place and carry on the business of the Lodge.

If the specified meeting place is outside the jurisdiction in which the Lodge regularly meets, i.e. in a different Province, a dispensation is required from both of the authorities concerned.

In the case of a peripatetic Lodge that seldom meets at its fixed Venue (such as a Provincial Stewards Lodge that rotates its meeting place), the procedures will be well practised by them in accordance with the above principles.

6.2 Lodge Dates

6.2.1 Regular Meetings

The dates for Lodge meetings are to be as stated in the Lodge by-laws. The by-laws will specify all the 'Regular Days'.

Other rules relating to meeting dates apply the following constraints:-

- The Lodge has no power to cancel or adjourn any Regular meeting. If the Lodge cannot meet on a regular day for any reason, it must obtain a dispensation to hold that regular meeting within 28 days, before or after the proposed Regular meeting date. If no Installed Master is present to occupy the Chair, the meeting shall be abandoned and the fact recorded in the Lodge Minute Book. Depending on the circumstance, if an emergency occurs in Lodge, the Lodge may be closed or called off.
- The Lodge does not have power to change the specified date of any Regular meeting except by modifying its by-laws or as described below.
- The Lodge does not have power to hold additional meetings unless it has obtained authority by means of a dispensation.
- No Lodge meeting may be held on Christmas Day, Good Friday, or a Sunday. These are classified as "Prohibited" days.
- If a Regular meeting falls on a "Prohibited" day, it can be re-arranged, without the need for a dispensation, for another day within seven days of the specified date (before or after).
- If a Regular meeting falls on a public holiday that is not a "Prohibited" day, it can either be held on the specified day or be re-arranged, without the need for a dispensation, for another day within seven days of the specified date (before or after).
- If a Regular meeting date needs to be changed for any other reason, it can be re-arranged for another day within twenty-eight days of the specified date (before or after). To do this the Lodge must obtain a dispensation.

6.2.2 Election and Installation Meetings

The by-laws will also identify the annual 'Election Meeting' and the 'Installation Meeting' which are to be held as consecutive Regular Meetings.

The date of the Installation Meeting generally though not necessarily determines the Lodge financial year being the date when Lodge Subscriptions become due (or possibly 1st of Installation Month). It also sets the start of the 'Lodge Year' e.g. 2009-2010 or 2010-2011.

The Regular Election Meeting date cannot be changed without a change to the by-laws or other reason described above.

The Regular Installation Meeting date is subject to the same constraints but may change in some circumstances e.g. if the Master Elect dies (see Chapter 6.3.10) or his Election becomes Void (See Chapter 9.4.1).

6.2.3 Emergency Meetings

Emergency meetings of the Lodge may be called for any good reason (to be agreed as such and sanctioned by means of a dispensation).

These reasons may include but are not limited to dealing with major issues of urgency such as carrying out additional Ceremonies; Death of a Master or Master Elect; issues relating to a change in the Lodge by-laws; issues relating to Lodge Finances.

Emergency meetings are to be summoned by the Master, or if not available the Senior Warden, or if not available the Junior Warden. They cannot be convened without authority.

They should only be convened if it is deemed that the whole Lodge should be involved, rather than just members of the Lodge Committee.

Other rules relating to Emergency meeting dates apply the following constraints:-

- Not more than one meeting of a Lodge may be held on one and the same day.
- No business designated by the *Book of Constitutions* to be transacted only at a regular meeting shall be transacted at an emergency meeting.
- An emergency meeting shall not include any business whatsoever except such as is mentioned on the summons convening the meeting.
- No minutes of any previous meeting are to be read or confirmed at an emergency meeting, except in so far as any such minutes relate to or affect the validity of the business so mentioned.

6.3 Lodge Officers

This section looks at the role and duties of those Lodge Officers that require the Lodge Secretary's awareness, attention, advice or action. The election and installation of the Master and the investiture and appointment of officers are covered in Chapter 8.

6.3.1 Regular and Additional Officers

The *Book of Constitutions* is specific with regard to the number and titles of Lodge Officers. It states that the Officers listed below will or may be appointed "…**but no others**…".

Regular Officers	Required Additional Officers	Optional Additional Officers
Master	Almoner	Chaplain
Senior Warden	Charity Steward	Director of Ceremonies
Junior Warden		Assistant Director of Ceremonies
Treasurer		Organist
Secretary		Assistant Secretary
Senior Deacon		Steward(s)
Junior Deacon		
Inner Guard		
Tyler		

This means that unless and until the Rules are amended the Chief Steward, Dining Steward, Assistant Treasurer, Events Organiser, Mentor or Royal Arch Representative cannot be appointed as Officers.

In reality this means that where deemed necessary or appropriate, Lodge members fill these other roles but do not hold an "office".

Brethren who are not "Officers of the Lodge" should not be appointed as such by the Master at his Installation nor listed on the summons as Officers. The "Investiture and Appointment of Officers" being concluded, the members filling these other roles could be presented by the Director of Ceremonies and thanked by the Master for their contribution and work.

No brother who holds a Regular Office can hold more than two offices at any one time, only one of which can be a Regular Office.

A Brother who does not hold a Regular Office is not constrained on the number of additional offices he holds.

The Immediate Past Master is not a Lodge Officer. He holds his position and responsibilities by virtue of his Mastership. It follows that as he is not an Officer he is eligible to hold a Regular and/or an Additional Office.

A brother who is not a subscribing member of a Lodge may only hold the office of Tyler. This means that a non-subscribing organist is not an Officer of the Lodge.

The rule affecting emoluments also applies e.g. a non-subscribing Organist or Tyler can be paid whereas a subscribing Organist or Tyler cannot be paid.

6.3.2 Master

The Lodge Secretary is appointed to his office annually by the Master. The effectiveness of the Secretary greatly affects the manner in which the Master rules and directs his Lodge and therefore has a strong influence on its harmony and happiness.

There are many instances where the *Book of Constitutions* specifically requires that the Master complies with its rules. The Secretary is either directly or indirectly involved with nearly all these occasions. As an example, a Master tells his Secretary that "We cannot find the Warrant – what shall we do?". (See Chapter 10.3).

This sort of example reinforces the need for the Secretary to always have the *Book of Constitutions* and *Information for the Guidance of Members of the Craft* to hand at Lodge Meetings. Attendance at Secretaries' Seminars are also useful to find how the Secretary's own Province deals with the "We don't have our Warrant" phone call.

The list of Master-related items that either do or could require Secretary input are as follows:-

B of C Rule	**The Master…**	**The Secretary's Role**
101	...may not open Lodge without a Warrant	Advise on interpretation of B of C and take Action
105(a)	…is to be balloted or declared	Prepare for declaration or ballot
105(b), (c)	… is to be installed	Prepare for Installation, produce Installation Returns for signature.
107	...to continue in office	Prepare for continuation, produce Installation Returns for signature
109	…must have served at least one year as warden	Check that any Candidate for Master has served at least one full year as warden
111	…must have taken obligation	Check if Master Elect will take the obligation or recite it (if he has already been Master of this or another Lodge).

B of C Rule	The Master…	The Secretary's Role
114	… is responsible for the due observance of the laws by the Lodge over which he presides	It is the responsibility of the Secretary to make the Master aware of the rules at the appropriate time
115	…can serve as Master for no more than two years unless by dispensation	Inform the Master as necessary - obtain dispensation if required
116	…will appoint officers except Master and Treasurer and Tyler	Advise on selection of officers if requested, interpretation of B of C and take Action
117	...must not be a proprietor or manager of tavern … where the Lodge meets	Advise committee, Master Elect or Master - obtain dispensation if required
118	...attend with his Wardens to summons by Grand Master	Assist in compiling required documentation or evidence
120	...remove officers	Advise Master, if asked, on his rights and impact on Lodge of alternative courses of action
122	…must give way to official visitation	Report to Master official visitation and any known intentions of Official Visitor vis à vis taking the chair.
125	…must make enquiries of visitors from other constitutions	Advise the Master of his duties and make enquiries if requested

B of C Rule	The Master…	The Secretary's Role
126	…can refuse admission to visitors	Advise brethren and report to Master when deemed necessary to exercise his right to refuse admission
138	…is to receive copy of by-laws at installation	To ensure that a copy of the Lodge by-laws is available
139	…may direct alternative days if meetings fall on prohibited days	to discuss alternative dates, and to notify Brethren
140	…can summon an emergency meeting	To advise Master on requirement and to send out Summons
141	… can cause a Motion for Removal of Lodge (relocation)	Advise on interpretation of B of C and take Action
141	…can apply for dispensation for temporary removal	Advise on interpretation of B of C and take Action
142	…can apply for dispensation for removal for one meeting	Advise on interpretation of B of C and take Action
143	…has ownership of all Lodge Property, in Trust for the members – if vested in special Trustees.	To inform Master what is Lodge Property and where it is. To take action required by Master

B of C Rule	The Master…	The Secretary's Role
144	…is to record Minutes of Lodge meetings or cause to be recorded by Secretary	To prepare minutes of Lodge Meetings for confirmation and signature by Master.
146	…must sign Annual Returns	Check Annual Returns against Membership and present to the Master for signature
151	…must sign Installation Returns	To prepare Installation Returns and present to the Master for signature
154	…can preside ex officio over any Lodge Committee	To liaise with Master concerning all Lodge Committee meetings, keep minutes and monitor action
156	...shall give a second or casting vote if votes are equal	Advise Master on his duties
160	…may sanction initiation in case of urgency	Determine the cause of urgency, advise the Master of B of C rules and prepare for initiation of candidate.
164	…may sign Certificates for candidates for initiation or joining	Ensure Application Forms are complete and have clarity regarding occupation. Present for signature.
165A	… may certify non-indebtedness of members - Transfer of membership on Amalgamation	Prepare Certificate for each member wishing to join Amalgamating Lodge, check with Treasurer and pass to Master for signature.

B of C Rule	The Master...	The Secretary's Role
173(a)	...may request other Lodge to perform Passing or Raising ceremony - conferment	To discuss programme with Master, committee and candidate; write to other Lodge Secretary on behalf of Master requesting conferment
179A(b), (d)	...must report convictions of members under 179A(a)	Report to the Master any convictions of which the Secretary is made aware; Advise Master of his duties.
180	...can formally admonish bad behaviour	Advise Master on his rights
277(a), (c)	...must appear at Grand Lodge with Wardens for Appeal against Erasure	Assist in compiling required documentation or evidence.

6.3.3 Treasurer

The Treasurer is the only Lodge Officer, apart from the Master, who is elected by a secret ballot of the Lodge members.

There is no Lodge Officer designated "Assistant Treasurer" because a Treasurer cannot delegate responsibility for the management of Lodge Funds. The Treasurer must sign all cheques. Moreover in view of the fact that there is specific provision for the election of a temporary Treasurer, an "Assistant Treasurer" should be unnecessary.

Along with the Secretary, it is the Treasurer who administers the affairs of the Lodge. The roles of the Secretary and Treasurer are closely associated with about 75% of the information used by the Secretary being shared with the Treasurer.

Many of the administrative actions take by the Secretary have to go via the Treasurer as finances are involved with registration forms, dispensations and Annual Returns.

In a similar way, many of the Treasurer's actions are subject to action by the Secretary both on the summons and in the Lodge. These range from his election, resolutions for changes to bank accounts and changes in subscription levels to submission and acceptance of annual accounts.

Whilst it is not the direct responsibility of the Secretary to check the activities of the Treasurer, as the Secretary is administering the Lodge in accordance with the *Book of Constitutions*, the timing and manner of execution of the Treasurer's activities form an important part of the Secretary's role.

If the Secretary is uncomfortable about how the Lodge financial affairs are being managed, the following checklist should provide a yardstick as to whether his concerns are warranted.

The Secretary should first go through the list with the Treasurer as he is probably in the best position to assess the situation, satisfy himself and offer help and advice to prevent problems escalating.

Depending on the response and outcome, The Secretary would be advised progressively to contact the Master, the Lodge Committee, the Visiting Officer and finally the Metropolitan, Provincial or District Grand Secretary.

The following check list is based on the B of C Rule 153 and the *Information for the Guidance of Members of the Craft* and provided the Secretary is satisfied with the answers, should serve as a good indicator that financial matters are in order.

Lodge financial management Check List

1 The Treasurer shall receive the books of Account together with all Lodge funds and property from his predecessor upon his investiture.

2 All Lodge moneys shall be paid or remitted to the Treasurer direct.

3 Treasurer shall deposit the same in an account in the name of the Lodge.

4 The bank in which the account is held is to be approved by resolution of the Lodge.

5 The Treasurer is to make all payments authorised or sanctioned by the Lodge.

6 All cheques must bear the signature of the Treasurer and (unless the Lodge resolves to the contrary) of at least one other member authorised by the Lodge.

6a *Where cheques require two signatures, a member authorised is under a duty to satisfy himself that the sum stated in every cheque he is called upon to sign is due from Lodge funds.* (*Information for the Guidance of Members of the Craft*)

7 The Treasurer shall regularly enter a full record of all moneys passing through his hands in the proper books of account.

8 At a pre-determined date, he shall prepare annual accounts showing the exact financial position of the Lodge.

9 The statement shall be verified and audited by a Committee of members of the Lodge annually elected for that purpose.

9a *The Audit Committee should comprise senior members and, whenever possible, with some knowledge of accountancy. The appointment of only junior members to the Audit Committee is disapproved (by Grand Lodge) and should be discontinued.* (*Information for the Guidance of Members of the Craft*)

10 Copies of the accounts and of the certificate signed by this Audit Committee that all balances have been checked and that the accounts have been duly audited shall be sent to all members of the Lodge together with the summons convening the meeting at which they are considered.

11 Such meeting shall be not later than the third after the date to which the accounts are made up.

12 The books of account shall be produced for inspection in open Lodge at such meeting, and on any other occasion if required by a resolution of the Lodge.

13 The same procedure of *annual accounts, audit and presentation* to members of the Lodge shall be followed in relation to any other funds maintained by or in connection with the Lodge (whether by the Treasurer or by a Charity or other Steward) for:-

  13a Lodge Benevolent Funds.
  13b The funds of Charity or Benevolent Associations,
  13c Charity Box collections

14 The Books of Account shall be the property of the Lodge. The Books together with all Lodge funds and property in his possession shall be transferred to his successor upon investiture.

6.3.4 Secretary

The Role of the Lodge Secretary is covered in Chapter 2.

6.3.5 The Almoner

It is part of the Almoner's role to maintain contact with widows of past members and those members and families who are sick or distressed. There are a number of ways that the Secretary can provide support information to assist with this.

- Pass on information to the Almoner if he hears of any brother who is sick or distressed, information that is often forthcoming in response to a Summons or a follow-up telephone call.

- Report to the Almoner and/or the Lodge Committee when a brother has missed more than two or three meetings, particularly if apologies have not been received. Enquiries can then be made into the cause of absence and assistance mentoring or support offered if appropriate.
- Pass on information to the Almoner if he hears of any brother (or brother's close family member) who has died.
- Ensure the Almoner is made aware of any changes of Address of widows or past members.
- Occasionally enquire of proposer, seconder or Lodge friend about welfare of a brother who has been absent for a prolonged period and pass details to the Almoner, if appropriate.
- Accommodate the Almoner's Report on the Agenda for each meeting and on the Lodge Committee Agenda if requested.

6.3.6 The Charity Steward

The Charity Steward is largely independent in his activities and performs the important and difficult task of extracting charitable donations from the brethren on a regular basis.

He has to produce annual accounts for submission to the Lodge, in the same way as the Treasurer. The notes referring to the Treasurer in this respect apply equally to the Charity Steward.

The Charity Steward may call on the Secretary to distribute his 'call for funds' for the Master's list with the Summons. He should also be kept up to date with all contact details.

The Charity Steward should be aware and/or deal with each Petition for relief related to a member or past member of the Lodge or their dependants.

Every petition to the Masonic Charities submitted through a Lodge to which the petitioner belongs or belonged or by his dependant shall be considered by the Lodge. Every Lodge receiving such a petition shall forward it to the Charity concerned together with a report.

The Secretary should accommodate the Charity Steward's Report on the Agenda for each meeting and on the Lodge Committee Agenda if requested.

6.3.7 Members Under the Age of 25 Years

The Grand Lodge dues payable in respect of Registration Fee, and Grand Charity Contributions under Rules 269, 270 and 271 are reduced by 50% for any Brother under the age of 25. The amount of this reduction should be applied to the subscription collected by a Lodge from a Brother under the age of 25. This reduction will not affect his privileges under Rule 145.

6.3.8 Qualification/Disqualification for Office

All subscribing members are equally qualified to stand for election for the offices of Master (subject to the provisions of Rule 105) or Treasurer or make themselves available for any other office whether they pay Full, Non-dining or Under 25 subscription.

Notwithstanding the above no member is "entitled" to advancement in the Lodge. The appointment of all officers, with the exception of the Master, Treasurer and non-subscribing Tyler, remain at the entire discretion of the Master Elect.

6.3.9 Removal of Officers

Rule 120 states that if a Master is dissatisfied with the conduct of **any** of the Officers he can take steps to displace such Officer and appoint another. This would include the Treasurer or Tyler.

The removal must take place at a Regular Meeting and the Officer concerned must have been given at least seven days advance notice of the complaint. If a majority of the members present at the meeting believe that the complaint is well founded, the Master has the power to remove him and appoint another.

Rule 121 states that "*...If a Lodge office becomes vacant ...such office shall be filled ... by appointment or election as appropriate for the said office. The Brother so appointed or elected should not be serving a regular office in the Lodge when the vacancy occurred.*"

It is most unlikely that the Master would take any of the above actions lightly or without good cause. The Secretary may wish to advise the Master of any major rift or resignations that may follow such actions when considering alternative courses of action.

6.3.10 Death of Officers

Death of the Master

In the absence of the Master, the Lodge is to be summoned by one of the following in order of precedence subject to availability:

Senior Warden
Junior Warden
Immediate Past Master
Senior Past Master

In the absence of the Master, the Chair shall be taken by the following in order of precedence subject to availability:

Immediate Past Master
Senior Past Master who is subscribing member of the Lodge
Installed Master who is subscribing member of the Lodge

If none of the above is present the Senior Warden, or in his absence the Junior Warden, is to conduct the business of the Lodge but request an Installed Master to open and close the Lodge and confer degrees.

If no Installed Master is present at an appointed meeting, the meeting shall be abandoned and the fact recorded in the Minute Book.

Death of the Master Elect

If the Master Elect dies more than six weeks prior to the Installation meeting the Master may summon an emergency meeting to be held not less than three weeks before the Installation meeting to elect his successor. The Installation meeting is then to take place as normal.

If the Master Elect dies seven days or more prior to the Installation meeting a summons shall be issued to each member informing them of the fact and intimating that on the said day the Brethren will again proceed to elect a Master. The Installation meeting shall then be held within five weeks, by way of an emergency meeting if necessary.

In each of the above circumstances, the serving in office of Master and Wardens for one full year in accordance with Rules 9 and 105 shall be deemed to have been complied with.

If the Master Elect dies less than seven days before the Installation meeting the outgoing Master will continue in office for the period for which the Master Elect was elected and appoint and invest officers selected by the Master Elect.

Death of a Lodge Officer

If a Lodge office becomes vacant (other than that of Master) as a result of the death of a Brother or other cause, such office shall be filled for the remainder of the year by appointment or election as appropriate for the said office. The Brother, so appointed or elected, should not be serving a regular office in the Lodge when the vacancy occurred.

6.4 Lodge Committee

The Lodge Committee is established if authorised by its by-laws. The by-laws will state who are to be members, the terms of reference and the number required to form a Quorum.

The committee is charged with considering and reporting upon matters affecting the Lodge. It has no executive powers and must submit to the Lodge for consideration any matter that is deemed to be for its benefit.

The Master of the Lodge ex officio belongs to and is entitled to preside over every Committee of the Lodge.

Reference to the taking and recording of minutes is made neither in the *Book of Constitutions* nor the *Information for the Guidance of Members of the Craft*.

However, as anything beneficial to the Lodge emanating from the Committee is required to be put to the Lodge for its consideration, notes should be taken as a minimum.

Notes or minutes will therefore be taken or not at the request of the Master or in accordance with Lodge Custom.

It may be considered good practice to keep minutes provided that members' 'off the record' comments remain as such. Any meeting minutes assist in tracking the major decisions that need to be taken in a Lodge such as candidate interviews, changing venue, increasing subscriptions, Lodge programme, promotions or preparing for a Lodge Anniversary.

If formal minutes or notes are taken, they may be subject to surrender and or retention by the Grand Master or the Metropolitan, Provincial or District Grand Master as the case may be in accordance with Rules 74, 118 and 234.

6.5 Lodge of Instruction

The Lodge of Instruction is an important part of Freemasonry and is treated as such by Grand Lodge. The Secretary is not necessarily directly involved in the administration of the Lodge of Instruction but his advice on compliance with the *Book of Constitutions* rules may be required.

When it comes to promotions, attendance at Lodges of Instruction may be taken into account. If so, the Lodge Secretary needs to know if potential candidates for promotion are attending.

A Lodge of Instruction cannot be established or held unless it is "*...under the sanction of a regular warranted Lodge, or by the licence and authority of the Grand Master.*"

The meeting dates and venues have to be submitted to the appropriate Metropolitan, Provincial or District Grand Secretary for approval.

Minutes of Lodges of Instruction are to be kept recording attendees and the Brethren appointed to hold office. The minutes are to be produced when called for by the Grand Master, the Metropolitan, Provincial or District Grand Master, the Board of General Purposes, or the Lodge granting the sanction.

If the Secretary is aware that a Lodge of instruction has become inactive, he must take measures to ensure either that it becomes active again or go through the necessary steps for withdrawal of sanction. A Lodge of Instruction cannot just cease functioning.

6.6 Lodge Stationery

The quality of the paper and style of the documents produced by the Secretary serve to provide the first and ongoing impression of the Lodge to its members and its visitors alike.

It is the part of the duty of the Secretary to manage the Lodge stationery.

Fundamental factors such as weight of paper, colour, embossing, sharpness of printing and document layout are important in raising the quality of the documentation and the energy of the Lodge and its members.

The stock of stationery to be considered includes:-

- headed paper (logo only) can be used as continuation paper, agendas etc or for officers to incorporate their own address details. (80 - 100gsm paper).
- headed paper (addressed) for the Secretary and Treasurer. (80 - 100gsm paper).
- compliments slips (80 - 100gsm paper).
- Summons paper – If the summons is printed by the Secretary, Logos and other high definition information can be pre-printed professionally – leaving the Secretary to overprint the Agenda and other variable text. (90 – 120 gsm paper).

Many Secretaries now use computers for the production of their Lodge documentation. This means that headed paper can be generated by each Secretary or Treasurer if they have the computing skills and have a printer of good enough quality.

In addition, subject to the agreement of the individual Member or Masonic Authority, summonses may be sent by email "…where the Secretary of a Lodge was able and willing to despatch summonses by email…".

6.7 Production of Summons

The Grand Lodge has approved dispatch of summonses by email if requested either in writing or by email. Every member who has not asked for summonses to be sent by email must continue to receive it by post. At least one printed copy of each summons must be retained by the Lodge for its records. Any relevant Masonic Authority must be sent in printed form unless electronic transmission has been requested.

The distribution of the summons by email is the most economic option and in many ways very convenient both for the Secretary and the Lodge Member. However, there are certain exceptions.

- The member does not have a computer – summons has to be posted
- The member does not have broadband – if long download time, member may choose to receive summons by post.
- The member does not have the software to open the summons - summons has to be posted.
- The member does not have a printer to print it - summons has to be posted.
- The member does not have a colour printer or high grade paper to print the summons – The member will benefit from on screen information but a high quality summons should be available for him and his visitors at the Lodge meeting.
- As a general statement, if email is used for Summons distribution, it is prudent for the Secretary to bring an increased number of Summonses with him to the Lodge to ensure that both Members and Visitors have a summons on the required quality of paper and appearance. Over the course of several meetings, it will become apparent how many members require them on the night.

The production of a few extra summonses is more than offset by the cost and work benefits of emailing that also enables and encourages attendance responses from the members.

A summary of the methods of producing the Summons and their advantages and disadvantages is listed below:-

a) Manually change the last 'hard copy' and send it to the Print Shop.

Advantages	**Disadvantages**
Traditional method of dealing with summons.	Needs careful preparation, proof and final draft reading.
Should be professional quality.	Can be most expensive.

Can incorporate embossing and high colour	Summons has to be distributed by regular post.
	Sorting, envelope packing, labels and postage.
	Deadline for amendments 4-6 weeks before meeting.

b) Change the 'printer's template' on the Secretary's own computer and send the proof/disk to the Print Shop.

Advantages	**Disadvantages**
Should be professional quality.	Expensive - Similar to above - may be slightly cheaper
Can incorporate embossing and high colour	Summons has to be distributed by regular post.
Better control and recording of amendments	Proofreading more straightforward Sorting, envelope packing, labels and postage.
	Deadline for amendments 4 weeks before meeting

c) Secretary to change his own template and print the text onto pre-printed summons paper.

Advantages	**Disadvantages**
Common method of dealing of amendments	Secretary has to have good quality printer
Quality as good as pre-printed paper	Summons has to be distributed by regular post
Can incorporate embossing and high colour	
Total control of format and timing	Sorting, envelope packing, labels and postage

Deadline 3-4 weeks before meeting	Cannot be emailed as on pre-printed paper
Good control and recording timing	

d) Secretary to change his own template and print whole summons

Advantage	**Disadvantages**
Increasingly common method of dealing with summons.	Secretary has to have good quality printer
Quality as good as paper, design and printer	Summons has to be distributed by regular post
Can incorporate high colour	Sorting, envelope packing, labels and postage
Total control of format and timing and quality	Cannot incorporate embossing
Deadline 3 - 4 weeks before meeting	
Good control and recording of amendments	
Capable of sending by email	

e) Secretary to change own template, to send the summons out as an email document and for each member to print the summons for himself and his visitors.

Advantage	**Disadvantages**
Increasingly common method of dealing with summons.	Secretary has to have good quality printer
Lodge Version Quality as good as paper, to produce summons	Only applicable to Members who request Summons in Electronic Format

Can incorporate high colour	Member's Version Production & Quality dependent upon member's printer
Total control of format and timing and quality	Increased number of printed Summons taken to Lodge as back-up
Deadline 3 weeks before meeting	
Good control and recording of amendments	
Capable of sending by email	
Most Economic Solution	

Whichever method is used by the Secretary will doubtless be suited to himself and the Lodge. If a particular method has been used for a long time, meets the quality and financial requirements of the Lodge and is suited to the working methods of the Secretary, there is absolutely no reason to consider change.

CHAPTER 7

LODGE MEMBERSHIP

7.1 Generally

The Lodge Secretary's role with regard to 'People' is very much one of managing and communicating information, knowledge and wisdom.

A large part of the role is related to collecting, recording and using Personal and Masonic information about candidates, members, visitors and others. Historically all this information was stored in card indexes, schedules, lists, pre-printed labels, meeting minutes, attendance books, a wide range of Grand Lodge forms, box files, lever arch files, and much in the heads of successive Secretaries.

The computer age makes this activity simpler because a variety of word processing, spreadsheets, data bases and bespoke programs assist with easy access, selection, sorting, comparison and effective use of data.

Notwithstanding the amount of data gathered, stored and used, the vast majority of Lodges are not required to register as "data users" under the Data Protection Act.

In order to comply with the conditions of exemption from registration as a "data user" the Secretary should inform each Lodge member of the extent of information held on him and its purpose. He should include a statement that the information held will not be communicated to any third parties and that it will not be subject to any other automatic processing.

The Secretary should be aware that the information that is gathered and stored can be quite extensive and is often considerably more than the bare minimum. It is essential that this information is reserved for uses in connection with the running of the Lodge and that it remains confidential.

When each member is sent a copy of the information that is held on him, he can also be asked to add to or amend any facts that are outdated.

In addition to complying with Data Protection Act legislation, this serves to ensure that addresses, phone numbers and general Masonic information are kept up to date.

The Lodge Member should be asked to state if he does not wish the information to be included in address or telephone lists that are distributed amongst members and/or if he wants the information to be removed from the computer.

Whether computer based or not, the information gathered falls into two main categories – Personal and Masonic.

7.2 Personal Details

The following is a schedule of fields that can be used for manual, spreadsheet or data base management of the personal information that is required to be held on each member for the purposes of managing the Lodge. Each field is categorised as either 'Essential' or 'Optional'.

7.2.1 Personal Data Required for Lodge Management

Typical Field Names	Reason Data Required	Essential or Optional
Name and Address		
Title	*In support of key name data*	*O*
First Name	Registration Form	E
Other names	Registration Form	E
Familiar Name	*In support of Key name data*	*O*
Initials	Annual Returns	E
Surname	Registration Form	E
Qualification/Honorific	*In support of Key name data*	*O*
Date of Birth	Registration Form	E
Date of Death	Annual Returns	E
Marital Status	*In support of Contact Information*	*O*
Home Address 1	Registration Form	E
Home Address 2	Registration Form	E
Home Town	Registration Form	E
Home County	Registration Form	E
Home Post Code	Registration Form	E
Home Phone	Registration Form	E
Home Fax	*In support of Contact Information*	*O*
Home Mobile No	*In support of Contact Information*	*O*
Home Email	Registration Form	E

Typical Field Names	Reason Data Required	Essential or Optional
Special Needs		
Special handicap needs	*Organise Transport, Lodge & FB*	*O*
Special meals	*Arrangements at Festive Board*	*O*
Family		
Wife/Partner Status	*In support of Contact Information*	*O*
Wife/Partner Title	*In support of Contact Information*	*O*
Wife/Partner name	*In support of Contact Information*	*O*
Wife/Partner Surname	*In support of Contact Information*	*O*
In touch with Widow/Partner	*Almoner, Contact Widow*	*O*
Widow/Partner Phone No	*Almoner, Contact Widow*	*O*
Business		
Occupation	Registration Form	E
Employer	Registration Form	E
Business Address 1	Registration Form	E
Business Address 2	Registration Form	E
Business Town	Registration Form	E
Business County	Registration Form	E
Business Post Code	Registration Form	E
Business Phone	*In support of Contact Information*	*O*
Business Fax	*In support of Contact Information*	*O*
Business Mobile No	*In support of Contact Information*	*O*
Business Email	*In support of Contact Information*	*O*

Essential and Optional Personal Information

The 'Essential' information is quite straightforward and its need and use should be clearly understood.

However, 'Optional' Personal information has to be used in a more circumspect and diplomatic manner, particularly by the incoming Secretary.

There are many issues around the keeping of personal data that have to be considered.

The use of computers makes complete sets of information readily and immediately accessible. Back-ups of the information can be stored on memory sticks, the size of a 'key fob', which can be easily lost.

If a memory stick containing every Lodge Member's personal, business and Masonic details fell into the wrong hands it could be used for a number of personally embarrassing or criminal purposes. It is recommend that such devices are used with extreme caution and not used habitually to transport Member data.

Particular care should therefore be applied to 'optional' Personal information as typified in the following examples:-

Familiar Name and Family Details

The Secretary must take into account that his predecessor may have saved information specific to **his** own relationship with any particular Lodge member and his family.

There is no requirement on the Registration Form for a Candidate to enter his Marital Status. However, it is usual during the interview to determine if the Candidate's family are happy with his joining Freemasonry.

Over the course of time, friendships are built that result in many first name conversations between the Secretary and the members' families. Knowing first names and surnames of partners is an important part of the stability of the Lodge and its members.

However, familiar names and names of family members should be used with caution by the new Secretary as a member, or one of his family, whilst being comfortable to be addressed in a familiar way by his predecessor may be concerned or offended about being addressed in the same manner by someone that they do not know. They may not realise that the Secretary's 'aide memoire' is now next to the address and masonic details on the Lodge data base.

Mobile Phone No

The Installation Return requests the mobile telephone numbers of the Almoner, Charity Steward and Secretary. For others, provision of a mobile telephone number, whilst not obligatory, is a most useful means of communication.

Special Handicap and Dietary Needs

Many members either have requirements related to some form of handicap or dietary needs or preferences. It is normal for the Secretary to know of these and to deal with the means of ensuring that each member's requirements are met.

Keeping in Touch with Deceased's Partner/Widow

It is part of the Almoner's role (See Chapter 6.3.5) to maintain contact with widows of past membersbers but it is normally the Secretary who has this information in advance of the demise of a Lodge Member. For continuity, the Lodge Secretary should carry on holding this information. The family address can be maintained under the deceased Member's name.

Business Contact Numbers

The Grand Lodge Installation Return requests the business telephone numbers of the Almoner, Charity Steward and Secretary. Many other members also provide business telephone numbers or email addresses. This information is not mandatory and when these forms of communication are provided, particular care should be taken to ensure that the Lodge Member's confidentiality is not compromised.

7.3 Masonic Details

The following schedule is not exhaustive but suggests the Masonic information that may be held on each member and whether Essential or Optional.

7.3.1 Masonic Data Required for Lodge Management

Typical Field Names	Reason Data Required	Essential or Optional
Masonic Identity		
Grand Lodge Computer Reference Number	Annual Returns	E
Grand Lodge Certificate Number	*In support of Masonic ID*	O
Metropolitan/Provincial/ District Reference Number	*Unique Metropolitan/Provincial/ District Identity*	O
Masonic Details		
Name of Proposer	Registration Form	E
Name of Seconder	Registration Form	E
Seniority in Lodge	*Lodge Management*	*O*
Rank Prefix	Form of address and hierarchy	E
Lodge Rank	Hierarchy and position in Lodge	E
Metropolitan/Provincial/ District Rank	*Form of address and hierarchy*	*O*

Typical Field Names	Reason Data Required	Essential or Optional
Grand Rank	*Form of address and hierarchy*	*O*
Lodge Committee Member	Committee Address List	E
Date Initiated	Registration/Returns Forms	E
Date Passed	Certificate Application	E
Date Raised	Certificate Application	E
Joining date	Registration/Returns Form	E
Founder/Joining	Registration/Returns Form	E
Resignation date	Grand Lodge Annual Returns	E
Cessation date	Grand Lodge Annual Returns	E
Rejoining date	Grand Lodge Annual Returns	E
Exclusion date	Grand Lodge Annual Returns	E
Country Membership date	Different billing	E
Honorary date	Grand Lodge Annual Returns	E
Offices Held		
Office Held	Installation Returns/Promotions	E
Period Held	Installation Returns/Promotions	E
Office Held Other lodge	Installation Returns/Promotions	E
Other Lodge number	Installation Returns/Promotions	E
Other Lodge name	Installation Returns/Promotions	E
Other Lodges and/or Orders		
Member of Other Lodge	If joining - required for Rule 163(c)	E
Past Member Other Lodge	If joining - required for Rule 163(c)	E
Other Lodge No	*Promotions, links and contacts*	*O*
Other Lodge Name	*Promotions, links and contacts*	*O*
Type of Lodge	*Promotions, links and contacts*	*O*
Title	*Promotions, links and contacts*	*O*
Rank	*Promotions, links and contacts*	*O*
MPD Rank	*Promotions, links and contacts*	*O*
Grand Rank	*Promotions, links and contacts*	*O*
Year in Chair	Installation Returns/Check Rule 115	E

Essential and Optional Masonic Information

Once more, the 'essential' information is straightforward with the need for the information loosely defined or referenced to specific *Book of Constitutions* clauses.

The context for which Masonic information is categorised as 'Optional' varies as clarified below:-

Metropolitan, Provincial or District Ref No.

Some Regions utilise their own numbering system, with others using the Grand Lodge Computer Reference numbers. If Regional Reference Numbers are used, these may be 'Essential'.

Seniority

Seniority in Lodge is determined by the latest date of becoming a member. This means that the chronological date and order of being initiated or joining sets the seniority but if one leaves and rejoins, it is the later date that determines the seniority.

Seniority is distinct from Precedence. 'Precedence' is determined by office and rank and not length of membership.

Metropolitan, Provincial and District Rank and Grand Rank

Masonic Promotion information is available from yearbooks and is useful for basic Lodge Management.

However, it is not unknown for members who have moved away and become active in another Lodge or Province to receive Masonic honours and not to communicate that fact to the Secretaries of the remaining Lodges to which they belong. There are no penalties for failing to report honours received. Attendance in Lodge will normally rectify this omission.

Membership of Other Lodges and Orders

Many members belong to other Lodges and other Orders both within the same Province and/or in other Provinces. The Secretary gets to know some of these other memberships by way of Registration Forms for joining, and requests for Clearance Certificates.

Other Lodge membership details are of interest and also useful in putting together a case to Province for a member's promotion. However the information is only 'Essential' in respect of:-

- Joining or Re-Joining Members who have to declare all their past and present Craft Lodge memberships; Constitution; date of admission; and year of Mastership (if relevant) on the Registration Form.
- Masters and potential Masters of other Lodges whose Masterships cannot overlap without dispensation.
- Masters and Past Masters of any other Craft Lodge where the information is reported on the Installation Return.
- Membership and Office details of any other Craft Lodge and/or Royal Arch Chapter, within the Province, where the information is required on Promotion Application forms.

Contacts
This information is optional as its extent is not defined and is not required to be in a finite form. However a comprehensive data base of contact names, addresses and phone numbers is a most useful tool for the Lodge Secretary and his successor.

7.4 Grand Lodge Registration Forms

7.4.1 Initiates

Initiation Generally
It is the Secretary's responsibility to administer the conditions and rules governing the eligibility and suitability of a candidate for initiation. He has to oversee or carry out the many actions required before the Initiation Ceremony can take place.

The Proposer and Seconder should be aware that they will be liable for all fees payable to the Lodge by their Candidate. (Rule 171).

The selection process for Candidates involves a number of stages intended to ensure that as far as possible the Lodge Members are happy with the Candidate joining their Lodge and being admitted into Freemasonry.

In a similar way, the selection process is intended to ensure that the Candidate is happy that he wants to proceed based on what he knows about his proposer, his seconder and other Lodge Members he has met; what he has already learned about Freemasonry; the commitments that have been explained to him and the documents he has signed.

The following comprises a check list of rules and actions leading to the decision that the Candidate can proceed to the Initiation Ceremony

Eligibility of a Candidate for Initiation

Any candidate for initiation must be at least twenty-one years old (unless by Dispensation of the Metropolitan, Provincial or District Grand Master), and a free man of reputable character.

Any person wishing to become a Mason must be proposed and seconded at a regular Lodge meeting by subscribing or Honorary members of the Lodge. (Honorary members must be Past Masters of the Lodge to propose or second a Candidate). He must be well known to his Proposer and Seconder.

Before being proposed in open Lodge, the Candidate, his Proposer and Seconder have to complete the appropriate Grand Lodge Registration Form.

The Form must be completed giving the Candidate's full name, date of birth, home address and contact details, precise occupation, employer and business address details. (Poste Restante addresses and general occupation descriptions such as 'Company Director' or 'Civil Servant' are not sufficient).

The Form also includes a declaration by the Candidate. Ideally, the proposer and/or seconder or another Lodge Member at a preliminary or Lodge Committee interview will have determined that he is capable of giving positive responses to all the questions on his declaration. The Candidate must state the following:-

- if he has been proposed for membership in any other Lodge. This would include a previously submitted Application Form; his details appearing on a Lodge Summons for ballot; a preliminary interview by Lodge Members or Committee or any specific enquiry (of which he was aware) made by a Masonic Brother to any Lodge.
- that his application is voluntary.
- that he understands he must obey the laws of his Country.
- that he does not expect, anticipate or seek preferment or financial benefit by becoming a Mason.
- that he can freely declare himself a Mason provided that in doing so he is not seen to be pursuing business, professional or personal advantage.
- that he has not been convicted by a court; found guilty of dishonest or disgraceful conduct; disciplined by any professional, trade or other tribunal; nor is he awaiting the outcome of any proceedings at a criminal court or professional, trade or other tribunal.
- that he is not and has not been connected with any quasi–Masonic organisation regarded by Grand Lodge as incompatible or irregular with the Craft.

- that his declaration is true.
- that in compliance with the Data Protection Act he agrees to the processing of personal data and information by the United Grand Lodge of England.

Anything other than a positive answer does not necessarily vitiate his application but will warrant the attention of Metropolitan, Provincial or District Grand Lodge and may influence the brethren when balloting.

A copy of his declaration is handed to the Candidate.

The form also includes Certificates to be signed by the Proposer and Seconder giving details of how well and how long they have known the Candidate; that they have informed him of his financial and time commitments; why they feel he is "…a man of good reputation and well fitted to become a member of the Lodge." Though not a requirement, copies of their Certificates may be retained by the Proposer and Seconder.

The Master certifies that he is satisfied as to the character and qualifications of the Candidate preferably before the candidate is proposed in open Lodge but definitely before the Ballot is taken.

The Secretary certifies regarding any qualifications to the Candidate's declaration and compliance with Rule 158 (Location) as appropriate. Usually the Secretary's signature is added to the Form immediately after the Initiation Ceremony.

It is important that the Secretary carefully checks the Form before submission to satisfy himself that the foregoing information is in order and that the Registration Form is completed correctly and duly signed. He should keep a copy of the complete form for his own records.

The Form, completed by the Proposer, Seconder and Candidate, should be handed to the Secretary at least two weeks prior to the Lodge Meeting at which the proposal is made. This is to enable the Secretary to check the basic information. The date that the Application Form is returned normally sets the precedence of Candidates.

Location - A candidate for initiation who is neither resident nor has principal place of business in the locality must state in writing why he is seeking to be a candidate outside his locality and why he not seeking to be candidate within his locality. The answer is likely to be common to both including a particular friendship or affiliation with a School or group of colleagues.

The Secretary must write to the Province where the candidate resides or has his principal place of business and obtain written confirmation that the Province knows of no reason why the candidate should not be considered for membership of the Lodge.

The *Book of Constitutions* states in Rule 158 that:-

"A candidate coming within the provisions of this Rule shall not be proposed in open Lodge until the Masonic Authority has replied to the enquiries."

If there is no adverse report from the said Province, the Secretary reports that Rule 158 has been complied with.

If reasons are stated by the said Province as to why the Candidate should not be considered, the Proposer and Seconder should be approached and given the option of withdrawing their proposal. If they still wish to proceed, the letter from the said Province must be read out in Open Lodge before the Ballot is taken.

Suitability of Candidate

The prime purpose of Rule 154 is to enable Lodges to include in their by-laws provision for forming a committee for interviewing candidates prior to Ballot. Interviews can be carried out either at Lodge Committee meetings and/or by two Past Masters visiting the candidate's home, either shortly before or after the completion of the Application Form.

The purpose of the interview is to ascertain the suitability of the candidate including:

- Ensure that the candidate believes in a Supreme Being.
- Find out whether the candidate's family is supportive of his entering Freemasonry.
- Determine whether the candidate is law abiding.
- Ask why the candidate wants to enter Freemasonry.
- Let the Candidate see other Lodge Members.

It is beholden upon the Lodge Committee, when interviewing the proposed Candidate, to enquire if he has any convictions or court hearings pending. Ideally this should have been determined, prior to interview, by the Proposer or Seconder.

If the candidate is unable to make an unqualified declaration that he has not been convicted of a criminal offence or has no court hearings pending, the Secretary should obtain relevant details and report them to Metropolitan, Provincial or District Grand Lodge for further advice.

The Lodge Committee cannot ballot for the candidate but can advise the Proposer and Seconder if they believe a ballot for the candidate would prove successful, or unsuccessful, in Lodge.

If any member has concerns about a Candidate, whether aired in the committee meeting or not, he should approach the Master or the Secretary to discuss his concerns before the ballot is taken in order to avoid the embarrassment of an unsuccessful ballot. It would be appropriate for the Secretary (or the Master) to occasionally remind the brethren of this obligation.

If in the view of the Lodge Committee the candidate is deemed suitable, the Secretary can report such to the Lodge, prior to the ballot taking place.

Proposal of a Candidate

The Candidate interview can take place either shortly before or after the completion of the Registration Form. Ideally, the interview should take place before the Proposal in Open Lodge but it may also be done at some later stage, before the preparation of the Summons announcing the Ballot.

Details of the Candidate must be included on the summons prior to Ballot, including name, address, occupation, date of birth and whether Rule 158 is complied with regarding locality.

A proposal for each candidate must be read in Open Lodge at a Regular Meeting.

The *Book of Constitutions* Rule 159 states that "*The particulars required of the candidate, as well as of his proposer and seconder, shall be furnished to the Secretary of the Lodge, previously to the meeting of the Lodge at which the proposal is to be made.*"

Notwithstanding the need for the completed application form to be with the Secretary before the meeting when the Proposal is read out, it is not unknown for Lodge Members to deliver a Registration Form on the day of the meeting.

This is not acceptable because although the Proposer and Seconder may have every confidence in their Candidate, it is not until he has completed and signed his declaration that the necessary details are available and that the Secretary can be assured that the Registration Form meets the requirements of Grand Lodge.

If any criminal details are revealed on the Form, these must be referred to Metropolitan, Provincial or District Grand Lodge Secretary who will either deal with them or refer them to Grand Lodge.

If the proposed Candidate lives and works in a different Province to that in which he seeks to be initiated, investigations must be made and the proposal cannot be read out in open Lodge until responses have been received from the appropriate Metropolitan, Provincial District Grand Secretary. Rule 158 applies

If any adverse comments are received, these must not be included on the summons but must be read out in open Lodge prior to any ballot.

The Secretary must insist that Registration Form is properly completed and signed by the Proposer, Seconder and Candidate before he reads the Proposal in Open Lodge.

The Master has to sign the Registration Form that should be done preferably before the Proposal in Open Lodge but definitely before the Ballot. If this has not been done prior to the meeting, the Secretary should ensure that he obtains the Master's signature prior to reading out the details for the Ballot.

Once the Proposal has been read out in Open Lodge and recorded in the Minutes, the process moves on to the Ballot.

Ballot of the Candidate

Ensure Master has signed the Candidate's Application/ Registration Form before the Ballot is taken.

The ballot for a Candidate must take place at the Regular Meeting following that in which the Proposal was read out in Open Lodge.

If the ballot is not held at the next meeting for some reason, the Proposal should be read again in Open Lodge and recorded in the minutes in order that it does not lapse. The Ballot can then be taken at the following Regular meeting.

If the Proposal and Ballot are not carried out at consecutive Regular Meetings, then the election is void and no ceremony can take place.

The Initiation Ceremony can take place immediately after the Ballot, at the same meeting, or up to one year after the Ballot. If the period between Ballot and Ceremony exceeds one year, then the Ballot becomes void and a second proposal and ballot would have to take place.

It is not uncommon to Initiate Candidates at the same meeting as the ballot is taken. However, this could be unwise if there is perceived to be anything less than unanimity in the Lodge regarding the Proposer, the Seconder or the Candidate.

An unsuccessful ballot resulting in a candidate being sent home due to rejection is embarrassing for all and would cause the most severe disharmony in the Lodge.

The Secretary should be aware of what constitutes an unsuccessful Ballot result in accordance with the by-laws of his Lodge. This is invariably between one and three black balls to exclude.

If the Ballot immediately precedes the Initiation and is successful, the Candidate must sign the Declaration Book subsequent to being successfully balloted and prior to being admitted for Initiation. The Secretary should leave the Lodge or determine from the Tyler that the book is signed and announce such to the Lodge prior to admitting the candidate.

If the Initiation Ceremony is to take place at any time other than immediately after the Ballot, the Secretary is to write to the Candidate informing him of the result and, if successful, details of when the Initiation ceremony is to take place.

Unsuccessful Ballot of Candidate

If the Ceremony was to immediately follow the Ballot, which proved unsuccessful by a single ball, after checking the by-laws for the required number of black balls to exclude, it is suggested that a further ballot takes place lest any member placed a wrong ball in the bag or a ball in the wrong box in error.

If the result is still unsuccessful after the second ballot, there may be disharmony in the Lodge and if the Master seeks advice, the Secretary could suggest any or all of the following:-

- The Secretary withdraws with the Proposer and/or Seconder and advises the Candidate of the result of the Ballot and that there will be no ceremony. The Proposer and/or Seconder remain with the Candidate if deemed necessary.
- If the Proposer is either Master or one of his Wardens, it might be appropriate to suggest that a substitute temporarily occupies his Chair whilst he attends to his Candidate.

If the Ballot is unsuccessful and the ceremony is not held at the same meeting as the Ballot, the Secretary should write to the Candidate informing him of the result and advising that if he applies to become a Mason again, he will have to declare his application that was unsuccessful.

After the meeting, efforts should be made to ascertain whether the cause of the failure of the Ballot was due to personal animosity to the Candidate or some other reason which, had it been known previously, would have disqualified the Candidate.

There will be a distinct possibility of resignations as a result of the rejection of a Candidate by an unsuccessful Ballot. The possible background reasons for the failure and why there was no prior warning, together with the personalities involved are all likely to influence the extent of the impact on the Lodge.

Preparation for the Initiation Ceremony

The necessary actions to be taken by the Secretary in preparation for the Initiation Ceremony are as follows.

- The item on the Summons relating to the announcement of the Ballot and Ceremony should include the following information:-

  "To ballot for and, if elected, Initiate (at a subsequent meeting) Mr.(name in full); Age; Profession or occupation (proper description); Private address; Business address; Proposer and Seconder; Date Proposed in Open Lodge; Rule 158 complied with. (if relevant) and the date of any ballot if held at a previous meeting."
- Send letter sent to Candidate advising of success of ballot, dress code, venue, time and date of Initiation Ceremony. Send copy to his Proposer.
- Notify Candidate of Fees and Subscription payable and ask Treasurer to prepare bill for Candidate.
- Ensure copies of the *Book of Constitutions, Information for the Guidance of Members of the Craft, Masonic Charities* and Lodge by-laws are available to present to the Candidate.
- Ensure any Grand Lodge or Provincial Training or Information Booklets or Lodge Information Booklets are available to present to the Candidate.
- The Candidate must sign the Declaration Book subsequent to being successfully balloted and prior to being admitted for Initiation. The Secretary should determine from the Tyler and announce to the Lodge that this has been done prior to admitting the candidate.

Post Ceremony Action

After the Ceremony the Secretary should address the following:-

- Remind Director of Ceremonies or Tyler to pass card with Second Degree Q and A to Candidate.
- Secretary to sign Application/ Registration Form.
- See that Treasurer receives payment for Initiation and Membership. Obtain cheque for Registration Fee from the Treasurer.
- Immediately send the Registration Form to Metropolitan, Provincial or

District Grand Lodge with Registration Fee. This serves two purposes. It allows Grand Lodge sufficient time to check the details of the Candidate before a Grand Lodge Certificate is issued. Secondly, if the initiation is in November or December, it avoids having to pay a higher Registration Fee, that increases on 1st January.

Initiation of Serving Brethren

It is very rare now that this Rule is called upon and a Dispensation is required in every case in accordance with Rule 170.

There are no fees due in respect of a Candidate for Initiation if he is serving and is initiated into the Lodge in which he is to serve, or by dispensation if he is initiated into any other Lodge under the Grand Lodge. His initiation has to be specially notified to Grand Lodge where his registration will be free but he will be charged for a special Grand Lodge Certificate.

Initiation of a Lewis

One of the delights in Freemasonry is the occasion when a father is joined in the Lodge by his son, known as a 'Lewis' . It is particularly pleasing when the father takes a key part of the ceremony. The *Information for the Guidance of Members of the Craft* defines a Lewis as *"...the uninitiated son of a Mason and it matters not whether the son was born before or after his father became a Mason."* There is no mention of a Lewis in the *Book of Constitutions.*

The only privilege that a Lewis enjoys over a 'non-Lewis' is that "...where a Lewis is one of two candidates being initiated on the same day he would be the senior for the purpose of the ceremony." There is no precedence over previously initiated candidates nor is there any waiver on the age requirement as stated in Clause 157.

7.4.2 Ceremony of Passing

The Ceremony of Passing involves the least work for the Secretary. The items that he has to attend to are as follows:-

- Ensure that there is a gap of at least four weeks between Initiation and Passing. Extra care should be taken with this Rule if the candidate is to be passed in another Lodge. If the ceremony takes place in a lesser period the ceremony shall be void unless the Grand Master grants a retrospective dispensation.

- No more than two candidates can be passed in the same Lodge on the same day unless by dispensation.
- The summons should include the full name of the Candidate and the date of his Initiation. If the Lodge has three or four candidates to be passed, the summons may list all their names and state "To pass two of ....".
- The Secretary should send a summons and a letter confirming dress code and the date, time and venue to the candidate. The Secretary is to ensure that a response is received to the summons.
- The Secretary may remind the Director of Ceremonies to provide the newly passed Brother with a copy of the Questions and Answers for the next ceremony.

7.4.3 Ceremony of Raising

The Ceremony of Raising involves a little more work than that for Passing. The items that the Secretary has to attend to are as follows:-

- Ensure that there is a gap of at least four weeks between Passing and Raising. Extra care should be taken with this Rule if the candidate is to be raised in another Lodge. If the ceremony takes place in a lesser period, the ceremony shall be void unless the Grand Master and the Board of General Purposes grants a retrospective dispensation.
- No more than two candidates can be raised in the same Lodge on the same day unless by dispensation.
- The summons should include the full name(s) of the Candidate(s) and the date(s) of their Passing Ceremony and if carried out in another Lodge.
- The Secretary should send a summons and a letter confirming dress code and the date, time and venue to the candidate. The Secretary is to ensure that a response is received to the summons.
- If it is Lodge Custom to present the new Master Mason with a Ritual Book, the Secretary should either obtain one or ensure that the Proposer has obtained one for presentation. Remind the proposer to ensure the candidate has a MM Apron.
- The Secretary of the Lodge in which the Brother was initiated is to apply to the Grand Secretary for a Grand Lodge Certificate.
- The Secretary should ensure that the Registration Form and Registration Fee were sent after the Initiation or no Grand Lodge Certificate will be issued.

7.4.4 Joining Members

Joining Generally

The process of proposing and electing a Joining Member is similar to a Candidate for Initiation and it is once again the Secretary's responsibility to ensure that all the conditions are complied with, that all necessary Certificates of Good Standing are obtained and the Grand Lodge Registration Form is correctly completed and signed.

Any Brother wishing to join the Lodge must be proposed and seconded at a regular Lodge meeting by subscribing or honorary members of the Lodge. Honorary members must be Past Masters of the Lodge to propose or second a Candidate for Joining.

Eligibility of Joining Member

Before being proposed in Open Lodge the Candidate for joining, his proposer and seconder are to complete the appropriate Grand Lodge Registration Form. When completed it should be handed to the Secretary previously to the Lodge Meeting at which the proposal is to be read out.

For any Brother to join a Lodge he must be a member of one or more Lodges and/or a past member of one or more Lodges, each from a Recognised Constitution. He must declare every such Craft Lodges of which he is a member and those that he has belonged to in the past.

From each Craft Lodge of which he is a Member he must produce a Certificate of Good Standing stating that he is not indebted to that Lodge. It is particularly important that the date on the Certificate is checked to see that it is not invalid.

From each Lodge that he has been but is no longer a member, he must produce a Certificate of Good Standing stating that he is not indebted to the Lodge. In addition the Certificate must state the circumstances in which he left the Lodge, and whether at that time all dues were paid, or have since been paid.

If such a Certificate is not available because the Lodge has closed, a Certificate must be obtained from the Grand Secretary stating the facts as they are known.

The Candidate for Joining must also produce his Grand Lodge Certificate for inspection by the Secretary. The Certificate bears his signature and includes the date of his initiation and the Lodge Name and Number in which he was initiated.

If the brother cannot produce a Grand Lodge Certificate because he is still an Entered Apprentice or a Fellowcraft, the Grand Secretary should be contacted to see if the circumstances warrant issue of a 1st or 2nd degree Certificate. Generally speaking, if he is still a member of the Lodge in which he was initiated, this is unlikely to be granted.

A brother can only join a Lodge if he can produce all of the above documents.

If the reports from past Lodges state a Brother has been excluded or has resigned without having complied with its by-laws the circumstances of such exclusion or resignation shall be stated to the Lodge before the ballot is taken, the better to enable the Brethren to exercise their discretion as to his admission.

If the Brethren are aware of the facts but still ballot in favour of the proposed Joining Member, then the Lodge "*...shall be liable for any arrears that may be owing by him to the Lodge or Lodges from which he has been excluded or has resigned.*(See Rule 163(d)).

The Proposer and Seconder should be aware that they will be liable for all fees (but not subscriptions) payable to the Lodge by their Candidate. (See Rule 171).

The Joining Member does not have to complete the full declaration required of the Candidate for Initiation. However if he is unattached he does have to verify that he has no convictions or pending criminal court, professional, trade or other tribunal proceedings.

The Form also includes Certificates to be signed by the Proposer and Seconder giving details of how long they have known the Candidate, and that they feel he is "*...a man of good reputation and well fitted to become a member of the Lodge*".

The Master certifies that he is satisfied as to the character and qualifications of the Candidate.

Rule 158, relating to Location, does not apply to Joining Members.

It is important that the Secretary checks the Form before submission to satisfy himself that all the necessary Certificates of Good Standing are valid; that he has seen the Candidate's Grand Lodge Certificate and that the Grand Lodge Registration Form is completed correctly and duly signed.

Usually his signature is added to the Form at the end of the meeting at which a successful ballot was taken for the Joining Member. The Secretary should keep a copy of the complete form for his own records.

Many Brethren who apply to join a Lodge have attended on numerous occasions, with their proposer who is a Lodge Member. The proposed Joining Member is therefore known to many Lodge members and in such circumstances an interview before the Lodge committee is not required.

For Joining brethren who are not so widely known, an informal meeting with the Master and one or two past masters should be sufficient to ascertain that the Candidate for Joining would fit in with other Lodge Members. The checks carried out by the Secretary should endorse any recommendation.

Once the Proposal has been read out in Open Lodge and recorded in the Minutes, the process moves on to the Ballot.

Ballot Joining Member

The Ballot for a Joining Member must take place at the next Regular meeting following that in which the Proposal was read out in Open Lodge.

If the ballot is not held at the next meeting for some reason, the Proposal should be read again and recorded in the minutes in order that it does not lapse and the Ballot taken at the following Regular meeting.

If the Proposal and Ballot are not carried out at consecutive regular meetings, then the election as a Joining Member is void.

If the Candidate is present at the meeting where he is to be balloted, it is normal for him to be asked to retire whilst the Ballot is taken.

If the Ballot is successful, the new Member will be admitted and congratulated and welcomed by the Master.

If the ballot is successful and the Joining Member is not present, the Secretary should write and inform him of the result of the Ballot and request the Treasurer to send him a bill for his Joining fee and his Lodge dues.

If the newly elected member does not attend for twelve months and has not paid either his joining fee or his dues, or taken up his membership in some other way, the election and his membership shall be considered void. Other ways may be considered as returning his attendance card (whether to attend or not), inviting a guest or proposing a candidate.

Unsuccessful Ballot of Joining Member

In the event of an unsuccessful ballot and the proposed Joining Member is waiting outside the door of the Lodge for the result of the ballot, it is suggested that a further ballot takes place lest any member placed a wrong ball in the bag or a ball in the wrong box in error.

If the result is still unsuccessful after the second ballot, there will be disharmony in the Lodge and if the Master seeks advice, the Secretary could follow all the steps as described above in "Unsuccessful Ballot for an Initiate".

Joining after being Initiated into a Serving Lodge

A Brother initiated as a 'Serving Brother' (with waived Fees) can be elected as a joining member of a Lodge.

Upon the first registration of a 'Serving Brother' as a joining member of a Lodge he must pay the same fee as an initiate. The Lodge will pay the initiate registration fee to Grand Lodge.

Once elected the Brother shall be entitled to full rights and privileges. He shall also be entitled to return his 'Special Grand Lodge Certificate' in exchange for a Grand Lodge Certificate of the same date as his original Certificate.

Joining Members from other Jurisdictions

If a Brother, seeking to join the Lodge, was initiated in a Lodge not under the Grand Lodge, the Lodge Secretary must ascertain from the Grand Secretary that the Constitution under which the Brother was initiated is recognised by the Grand Lodge.

Before being admitted as a member of the Lodge, the joining Brother has to make a declaration of adherence to the *Book of Constitutions* of the United Grand Lodge of England.

The Declaration must be made within twelve months of his election, be witnessed by a 'recognised' Brother and recorded in the Lodge Minutes.

A copy of the *Book of Constitutions* must be presented to each such joining Brother.

If the Lodge by-laws are so worded, the additional fees due to Grand Lodge as a result of coming from a different jurisdiction may be claimed from the Joining Member.

7.4.5 Re-Joining

If a Brother has been excluded, has resigned under Rule 183 or his membership has ceased under Rule 148, he may re-join the Lodge provided that he has settled all outstanding debts, both to the Lodge to which he is re-applying and to any other Lodge to which he is or has been a member.

The Secretary is to ensure that Grand Lodge has been notified of all outstanding dues having been settled.

The procedure for re-joining is the same as for a Joining Member, if having previously resigned under Rule 183 in good standing, in that he has to be proposed and seconded in Open Lodge and Balloted.

If the Re-Joining Member previously left the Lodge due to Exclusion or non-compliance with its by-laws or general regulations of the Craft, the reasons and circumstances of his having left the Lodge, and any other Lodge, need to be read in Open Lodge before the Ballot takes place.

On being accepted as a Lodge Member, his seniority in the Lodge is established by the date of his re-joining.

7.4.6 Election to Honorary Membership

It is not unusual for high ranking Officers of Metropolitan, Provincial or District Grand Lodge or Grand Officers, who have a particular affiliation with a Lodge, to have Honorary Membership conferred upon them.

It is advanced by Grand Lodge that exceptional Masonic Service should be the benchmark for election to Honorary Membership of a Lodge.

Honorary Membership of a Lodge should only be conferred on Brother *of "...good standing and worthy of such distinction by reason of his services to the Craft, or to the particular Lodge".*

An Honorary Member will not be liable for any fees payable to the Lodge but shall possess the right of attending the meetings of the Lodge.

However, he may not take any office in the Lodge nor make or vote on any proposition nor will his name appear on the list of subscribing members of the Lodge and if he is not a Subscribing Member of any other Craft Lodge, he may not attend the Grand Lodge (unless he is a Grand Officer).

If the honour is conferred upon a Past Master of the Lodge, he will have the same privileges and constraints except that he he may still propose or second Candidates for Initiation or Joining.

The Secretary should inform the Brother on whom it is proposed to confer the Honorary Membership of the above benefits and restrictions associated with the distinction. This should be done prior to the Ballot as he may not wish to lose some of the above privileges.

Nothing in Rule 127 relating to 'Disqualification to Visit' shall preclude a Brother's attendance at any Lodge of which he is an Honorary Member.

The Election of an Honorary Member is subject to a Ballot that requires three or more Black Balls to fail. This means that the Lodge by-law stating the number of Black Balls to exclude relating to Election of Candidates does not apply in this case.

Grand Lodge consider it inappropriate to have collective ballots for both subscribing and Honorary Members. However collective ballots for more than one honorary member would be in order.

If the Honorary Member is not at the meeting when his Ballot is taken, the Secretary should inform him by letter of the honour that has been bestowed upon him. The Secretary should also notify the Treasurer of the Honorary Member's status and that he will not be liable for any fees.

Particulars shall be given on the Annual Return of the date of a Lodge Member's election to Honorary Membership.

If an Honorary member is elected from another Jurisdiction, it is not necessary for him to complete the Declaration required of Joining Members from another Jurisdiction.

7.4.7 Country or Non-Dining Membership

Neither "Country Membership" nor "Non-Dining Membership" are defined or referred to in the *Book of Constitutions* or the *Information for the Guidance of Members of the Craft.*

The *Book of Constitutions* states that every subscribing Member is entitled to receive summonses and cannot be disqualified from holding office, by its by-laws or otherwise.

Rule 145 allows a Lodge in its by-laws to provide for a smaller subscription rate for *"…members who, for some cause satisfactory to the Lodge,are not in a position to enjoy such privileges regularly."*

The conditions that must prevail for a Member to be classified as a Country member are therefore defined in the individual Lodge by-laws and as such may vary.

However, the Standard by-laws issued by Grand Lodge provide the following 'Model' Clause as a guide:-

> **Non-dining or Country Membership**
>
> *"Any member who, for reasons acceptable to the Lodge, is not in a position to enjoy the privileges of the Lodge regularly may on written application to the Secretary and by resolution of the Lodge, be considered a non-dining or country member and shall pay a subscription annually in advance on 1st xxxx of such less amount than that provided for in by-law – 'Subscriptions' as the Lodge shall from time to time decide by resolution after notice on the summons at the previous regular meeting. When attending the Lodge and dining such member shall pay the current visitor's fee."*

It can be seen that the Model by-law requires a resolution and vote of Lodge Members for a member to be admitted to the 'Country List' . Some older existing by-laws may have more or less stringent requirements, such as no resolution required but a qualifying period of non-attendance for at least a year.

CHAPTER 8

DEPARTING THE LODGE

8.1 Generally

There are five ways that a Brother can cease being a member of a Lodge. They are:

1. Resignation
   - From the Lodge –Rule 183
   - From the Craft – Rule 183A
   - From the Craft – Rule 277A
2. Cessation Rule 148
3. Exclusion Rule 181
4. Expulsion by the Grand Lodge Rule 277 (i)
5. Death

Where the issue of outstanding dues is concerned there are a lot of similarities regarding Resignation from the Lodge under Rule 183, Exclusion and Cessation in that the following results are the same:-

- No Unqualified Certificate of Good Standing
- No Longer Member of Lodge
- Grand Secretary & Metropolitan, Provincial or District Grand Secretary made aware of indebtedness.
- Can pay and apply to rejoin in accordance with Rule 163

The difference between the three is that 'Resignation' (Rule 183) is in control of the Member, 'Exclusion' is in the control of the Lodge and 'Cessation' happens automatically in consequence of Rule 148 of the *Book of Constitutions.*

8.1.1 Disqualification to Visit

By ceasing to be a Member of a Lodge, various constraints are applied regarding visiting other Lodges. This is set down precisely in the *Book of Constitutions* as follows:-

Rule 127. In the case of a Brother who has ceased to be a subscribing member of every Lodge of which he has at any time been a member, the following provisions shall have effect, viz.

(i) If he comes within the provisions of this Rule by reason of his exclusion under Rule 148 or Rule 181, he shall not be permitted to attend any Lodge or Lodge of Instruction until he again becomes a subscribing member of a Lodge.

(ii) If he comes within the provisions of this Rule by reason of his expulsion from the Craft or by reason of his resignation from the Craft under Rule 183A or Rule 277A, his right to attend any Lodge or Lodge of Instruction shall be forfeited.

(iii) In any other case he shall not be permitted to attend any one Lodge more than once until he again becomes a subscribing member of a Lodge, and upon such one attendance he shall append the word 'unattached' to his signature in the attendance book, stating therein the name and number of the Lodge of which he was last a subscribing member.

Nothing in this Rule shall preclude the attendance of a Brother at any Lodge of which he is an Honorary Member.

8.2 Resignation

There are three levels of Resignation by which a Brother ceases to be a Member of a Lodge.

The first is his resignation from a Lodge in accordance with Rule 183 that is dealt with by the Lodge and reported on the Annual Returns to Grand Lodge.

The second is his resignation from the Craft whereby he no longer wishes to be known as a Freemason. This is dealt with by Grand Lodge.

The third is his resignation from the Craft after being invited to do so by Grand Lodge. This is also dealt with by Grand Lodge.

8.2.1 Resignation from The Lodge – Rule 183

If a Brother resigns from a Lodge, he does not need to seek the approval of the Lodge.

The resignation has either to be in open Lodge at a Regular meeting or in writing to the Secretary. The date of resignation will be either at the date of the meeting, from the date of receipt by the Secretary of the letter or at some future date stated by the member. In all cases the name of the Lodge Member and the date of his resignation are to be recorded in the Lodge Minutes.

A resignation under Rule 183, may be in the first instance by email. The notification will not be effective until the Secretary receives written notice bearing an original signature of the member. The written notice should then be deemed to have been received at the moment the Secretary received the email message. If the written confirmation is not received before the next regular meeting of the Lodge, the resignation must not be reported and the email message will be void.

If the resignation is by letter, the Secretary shall report it to the Lodge at the next meeting.

No acceptance of the resignation is necessary and it is irrevocable, with the following proviso.

- If, on notification of the resignation at a Regular Meeting, a majority of the Lodge Members present vote for the withdrawal of the resignation, the Resigning Brother shall have twenty-one days to reconsider. If he responds within this period that he wishes to withdraw his resignation, it shall be cancelled.
- If a Brother resigns after being served with a notice of Exclusion under Rule 181, the resignation cannot be withdrawn if the Lodge resolves to exclude the Member. If no vote is taken or the Lodge resolves not to exclude the member, the resignation may be withdrawn.

This clause seems complicated but reflects the deep thought put into the writing of the *Book of Constitutions.* It addresses the circumstance where a Brother is to be excluded for non-payment of dues and resigns in an attempt to avoid exclusion. He then has second thoughts and pays his dues and wants to withdraw his resignation – which he can do if majority of the brethren voting at the next Regular Meeting agree.

When a resignation is received by the Secretary or reported in open Lodge, the Secretary should notify the Treasurer and is to determine whether the Brother is indebted to the Lodge.

If he is indebted, the Secretary should write to the Brother, inform him of the situation, of his obligations and the consequences of non-payment of the amount due. This may be done in stages depending upon the circumstances of the resignation.

The resignation does not have to be reported to Grand Lodge or the Metropolitan, Provincial or District Grand Lodge except by recording the resignation on the Annual Returns and, if indebted, the date up to which the Brother is clear on the books.

Whilst no acceptance of the Resignation is necessary, it may be appropriate for the Secretary to write to the Brother on behalf of the Lodge sending its good wishes and/or regret, as directed by the Master.

Under Rule 175, a Brother is entitled to receive on request, free of charge, a certificate stating the circumstances of his leaving the Lodge and whether he is indebted or was indebted at the time of leaving and if/when the debt was discharged.

A Brother who has resigned may rejoin a Lodge by paying any outstanding dues, completing the necessary Registration Form, being proposed and seconded in open Lodge and balloted as in 7.4.5 above.

Any payment of outstanding dues must be reported to Grand Lodge immediately, if possible with a copy of the receipt and note of any amount still outstanding.

8.2.2 Resignation from The Craft – Rule 183A

If a Brother wishes to withdraw from Freemasonry altogether, he may write to the Grand Secretary and tender his resignation from the Craft, which includes Royal Arch Masonry.

The Grand Secretary will notify the Secretary of every Lodge and Scribe E of every Chapter of which the Brother is a Member and from the date stated, the Brother will no longer be a member of the Lodge or the Craft.

All matters relating to the Resignation from the Craft will be dealt with by the Grand Secretary.

If a Brother resigns under Rule 183A to avoid being the subject of Masonic disciplinary sanction, he shall not be entitled to resume any of the rights and privileges of a Freemason but shall be treated for all purposes as though he had been expelled from the Craft at the moment at which his resignation became effective.

A Brother who has resigned from the Craft may not rejoin Freemasonry or a Lodge unless he has gone through the necessary Grand Lodge procedures for the return of his Grand Lodge Certificate (and Grand Chapter Certificate) and The Grand Secretary is satisfied that his application to join or rejoin a Lodge is in order.

8.2.3 Resignation From The Craft – Rule 277a

If a Brother is invited to resign from the Craft by the Grand Secretary, it will be as a consequence of disciplinary action.

If the Brother resigns in writing to the Grand Secretary, "*...such resignation shall have the same effect as expulsion and shall take effect in the Craft and the Royal Arch (where appropriate) on the date of the receipt by the Grand Secretary of the letter of resignation.*"

The Grand Secretary will notify the Secretary of every Lodge and Scribe E of every Chapter of which the Brother is a Member and from the date stated, the Brother will no longer be a member of the Lodge or the Craft.

All matters relating to the Resignation from the Craft will be dealt with by the Grand Secretary.

8.2.4 Resignation of The Master

A Brother cannot resign his Mastership of a Lodge. He is obligated to serve until another is "...elected and installed in his stead..." at the next regular period of election.

Therefore, if a Master is unable or unwilling to complete his term of office or continue in office, he must resign from the Lodge thereby leaving the office of Master vacant.

If he did so, no other Master would be elected to replace him. Rule 119(a) will apply and the Lodge shall be summoned until the next regular period of election by the Senior Warden, Junior Warden, Immediate Past Master or Senior Past Master as available. In this case an Installed Master will be requested to occupy the Chair to open and close the Lodge and to confer degrees.

8.3 Cessation

The *Book of Constitutions* is very clear on the issue of Cessation. It states "*Should the subscription of a member to his Lodge remain unpaid for two years, at the expiration of that period he shall cease to be a member of the Lodge*".

"This Rule cannot be delayed or revoked by the Lodge."

The Rule has benefits for the member in that he cannot incur a debt greater than two years' subscriptions and for the Lodge in that its accounts cannot show increasing amounts of money owing that they may never receive. It also provides an absolute boundary as to when subscriptions have to be paid.

As the period for cessation is two years, the member should have had numerous requests for his subscription. The Secretary can take the following action:-

- Send a letter six weeks in advance of the Cessation date advising the Brother that unless he pays by the xxxx date, his membership of the Lodge will cease and the status of his departure will be as if Excluded by Vote.
- If no payment is received, the Secretary should report the Cessation to the Lodge and record the fact in the minutes together with the amount of dues owing.
- The Brother should then be advised that as from xxxx date, he is no longer a member of the Lodge and that his Cessation and his indebtedness have been reported to the Grand Secretary and also to the Metropolitan, Provincial or District Grand Secretary.
- Advise the member that he may not rejoin the Lodge without settling his outstanding debt and regular proposition and ballot in accordance with Rule 163 as in 7.4.5 above.
- Inform the Brother (if he is a past master and is not a member of any other Craft Lodge) that he is no longer a member of The Grand Lodge.
- Notify the Grand Secretary and the Metropolitan, Provincial or District Grand Secretary of the date of Cessation and the amount of indebtedness of the Brother to the Lodge.
- Remove the Brother's name from the Summons and from the circulation list.
- If the Brother pays some or all of the outstanding debt, report the same to the Grand Secretary and the Metropolitan, Provincial or District Grand Secretary.

A Brother whose membership has Ceased may rejoin a Lodge by paying any outstanding dues, completing the necessary Registration Form, being proposed and seconded in open Lodge and balloted as in 7.4.5 above.

8.4 Exclusion

Exclusion of a Brother by a Lodge under the provisions of Rule 181 can be a most serious matter as it is likely to involve allegations of bad faith as regards payment of debts or misbehaviour of some other form. It also has serious implications as regards his future involvement in Freemasonry in general.

The implementation of the Rule is public and precise and is separately identified for appeal and reinstatement in Rule 182.

It is therefore imperative that the Rules, carefully considered and put down in the *Book of Constitutions*, are adhered to by the letter to avoid any unnecessary repercussions.

A Brother may be permanently excluded from membership of a Lodge for any sufficient cause, provided the following steps are taken.

- Serve notice of 'Ballot for Exclusion' on the Member, by registered post or recorded delivery marked Private and Confidential to his last known address not less than 14 days before the meeting. The notice is to include details of the complaint and the time and date of the meeting.
- A certificate of posting should be retained to confirm the date of posting.
- Send a Notice of a 'Ballot for Exclusion of a Brother' (not to be named on the Summons) to be sent to Lodge members at their last known address not less than 10 days before the meeting. (This can be an item on the Summons).
- A certificate of posting should be retained to confirm the date of posting.
- The Brother will be able to put his case in writing or in person prior to the Ballot.
- The vote shall be by Ballot. If two thirds of those present vote in favour, the resolution to exclude will be carried and will be effective forthwith.
- The Secretary should record the result in the minutes together with the amount of dues owing.
- Inform Grand Secretary and the Metropolitan, Provincial or District Grand Secretary of the name of the excluded brother and the reason for his exclusion.

If a Brother resigns after receiving notice of 'Ballot for Exclusion', the Lodge must decide if it wishes to proceed with the Ballot because as set down above, the results of 'Ballot to Exclude' and 'Resignation' are very similar.

The only differences being that the Grand Secretary and the Metropolitan, Provincial or District Grand Secretary are not notified of the indebtedness immediately but are informed on the Annual Returns.

However, as the resigned member cannot receive any unqualified Certificate of Good Standing until he has paid his dues and the circumstances of his leaving the Lodge are declared, a Lodge may feel that this does not matter.

In both cases, a resigned or excluded member cannot rejoin without a Ballot of the Lodge Members.

Reinforcing the need to comply with Rule 181 to the letter, Rule 182(a) states *"If the Grand Master be satisfied that any Brother has been excluded without due cause or that the provisions of Rule 181 have not been complied with, he may, either of his own motion or on the complaint of the Brother who has been excluded, order him to be reinstated, and may suspend any Lodge which fails to comply with that order."*

8.5 Expulsion by The Grand Lodge

Expulsion of a Member is handled by the Grand Secretary.

Rule 175 – Grants of Certificates states "*Except as provided by this Rule no Lodge shall grant a Certificate of any kind to a Brother. In particular, a Brother who has been expelled from the Craft under Rule 277A shall not be granted a Certificate.*"

8.6 Death of a Lodge Member

8.6.1 Generally

The Secretary is normally the earliest in the Lodge to hear of the death of a member. This is an emotional time for friends and family and it is the Secretary's responsibility to ensure that matters affecting the deceased are handled with sensitivity and that communication with the family and the members of the Lodge cause no distress or offence.

The Secretary has to take following action relating to the deceased and his funeral:-.

8.6.2 Member and Funeral Details

The Secretary should garner the following information:-

Concerning	Information Detail	Nature or Use of Information
Deceased	Name of Deceased	Title name and rank
	Address of Deceased	For letters of condolence
	Date of Birth	Date
	Date of Death	Date
	Cause of Death	To answer enquiries

Concerning Funeral	Information Detail	Nature or Use of Information
	Date of Funeral	Date
	Time of Funeral	Time
	Location of Funeral	1st Gathering

Funeral	Concerning Information Detail	Nature or Use of Information
	Church Service	Yes/No
	Burial or Cremation	Burial/Cremation
	Location of Cremation	If different from 1st location
	Funeral Reception	Yes/No
	Location of Reception	House, hotel etc.
	Name of Undertaker	For further enquiries
	Address of Undertaker	If flowers are required etc.
	Telephone of Undertaker	To assist with enquiries
	Are Flowers required?	Yes/No
	Donations to?	Name of Charity

With the above information, the Secretary is in the position to answer any questions from the Brethren. If a Principal Officer dies, there are other issues that are covered in Chapter 6.

8.6.3 Death of Member Checklist

Once the Secretary hears of the death of a brother he should ensure that the following are notified as soon as possible:-

Master	Inform Master
Treasurer	Ensure no bills or reminders sent
Almoner	To attend to flowers/cards etc
Proposer	Closest in Lodge to deceased
Seconder	Closest in Lodge to deceased

Once the above brethren have been informed, some or all of the following actions should be taken, as appropriate:-

- Arrange ring around/ send email to members informing them of death of the Brother. (Funeral details may follow later)
- Ask Almoner to organise flowers and card to family.
- Inform all Brethren who may wish to attend the Funeral of details as soon as possible.
- Inform Secretaries of other Lodges of which Brother was a member.
- Ensure that a letter is sent on behalf of the Master and Lodge members expressing sympathy. (This may be done by Almoner).

- Almoner or Brother who was close to deceased to ascertain if assistance is needed.
- Include 'In Memoriam' on next Lodge Summons.
- Ask Brother who was close to deceased to give eulogy in Lodge. Send him print-out details of Deceased's Masonic Career.
- Inform Metropolitan/Provincial/District Grand Secretary of Brother's death
- Inform Grand Secretary of Brother's death.
- Arrange to collect any Lodge belongings from dependants - after appropriate interval.
- If Lodge regalia sold, deceased's family to receive money unless offered to charity.

CHAPTER 9

PREPARATION FOR LODGE MEETINGS

The visible mark of a Secretary's success is the smooth running of meetings. This section identifies the Secretary's background work in achieving this goal.

Whilst not always evident, much of the work that the Secretary does behind the scenes is fundamental to the continued existence and operation of the Lodge. As with many things in life, proper preparation is the secret of a quality finish.

9.1 Summons

9.1.1 GENERALLY

For most Lodges, the Summons has been developed over many years and its design and style have evolved to meet the needs and preferences of the Lodge members. The format and most of the content of the summons is in the hands of the Lodge.

When a Secretary produces a Summons that receives no adverse comments relating to punctuation, spelling, names, addresses and ranks he can congratulate himself, as at every meeting he has an experienced and critical team of 'proof readers' looking at the document for up to two hours.

In preparing the summons, before he even addresses the Agenda, the Secretary has to change all relevant dates, days, months and years; meeting numbers; names, addresses, and ranks; status and changes of membership.

Rule 104(a) defines the Lodge Officers and states that there should be "…no others." Lodge Officers should appear in their order of precedence which is defined in Rule 104(d).

The order in which the names of Honorary Members are to appear on the summons is set down in the *Information for the Guidance of Members of the Craft*. It states, inter alia, that "*…names should be shown in order of seniority of Masonic rank… the names of the Provincial and District Grand Masters, followed* *by their Deputies and Assistants, should ...precede ... other Brethren, with the exception of the M.W. The Grand Master and his Deputy and Assistant."*

9.1.2 In Memoriam and Eulogies

There is no definitive way for the reporting of the death of a Lodge Member.

However it is common practice to report the passing of a Brother by recording his name, date of death and age at the head of the 'Lodge Business' page of the Summons, enclosed in a box with a black border.

The Master usually refers to the passing of a Brother, immediately after the Lodge is opened.

A eulogy may then be given by a Brother who was close to the deceased after which the Brethren will stand in silence for a few moments in respect for departed merit. (See Chapter 8.6.3)

9.1.3 Dispensations

In exceptional circumstances, ceremonies and/or events may take place by Dispensation from the Grand Master or the Metropolitan, Provincial or District Grand Master after having paid the appropriate fees. Dispensations require to be read in open Lodge after the opening of the meeting or before the item that is subject to the Dispensation.

Dispensations may be applied for in respect of the following:-

B of C Clause	**Description**
90	Conferment of degrees at short intervals (Lodges Abroad) (**N.B.** Dispensation has to be obtained from Grand Master or District Grand Master)
109	Qualification of Warden for Master if serving less than 12 months
112	Election of Brother (not an officer) whilst Treasurer is temporarily ill or unavailable.
115	Master required to serve for more than two consecutive years. (No dispensation would be required if the cause of the third or subsequent year was as a result of implementing Rule 107 - Continuation in Office of Master or 108 Postponement of Installation of Master).
115	No Brother to be Master of two or more Lodges at the same time (**N.B.** Dispensation has to be obtained from Grand Master or in a District only by the District Grand Master)

B of C Clause	Description
117	Proprietor or manager of tavern or house taking office.
139	Meeting on alternative day
140	Convening an emergency meeting
141	Temporary removal of a lodge to a different location
142	Removal of Lodge to different location for one meeting
157	Initiate under 21 years old
168	Carrying out ceremony for more than two candidates on same day
170	Serving Brother initiated without fee
172	Degree ceremonies less than 28 days apart (**N.B.** No Dispensation is available in advance but the Grand Master may issue a retrospective Dispensation, otherwise the ceremony is void)
178	Public appearance in Masonic clothing
186	Meeting to discuss and resolve on the question of the formation of a Sovereign Grand Lodge. (**N.B.** Only applies to Districts – Dispensations from District Grand Master)
188	Lodge with less than five members (**N.B.** Dispensation has to be obtained from Grand Master).

9.1.4 Agenda

The Agenda should be prepared based on the following:-

- Work programme for the year
- Type of meeting (Regular, Emergency) ceremonies etc.
- Propositions, Ballots and Notices of Motion
- Presentations and Promotions
- Official visits
- Death of members
- Feedback from Lodge Committee meetings
- Correspondence from Grand Lodge and Metropolitan, Provincial or District Grand Lodge;
- Communications with the Master and other Lodge Officers

The wording of the 'Lodge Business' or 'Agenda' must comply with the rules contained in the *Book of Constitutions.*

Standard wording for all the items that will be required, in the correct order, is available from the Metropolitan, Provincial and District Grand Secretaries, most of whom monitor the wording on each summons.

The Secretary may produce a separate more detailed 'Working Agenda' that serves as a prompt for the Master (and Director of Ceremonies) identifying specific items that may not appear on the Summons, such as announcement of Eulogy, congratulating a Joining Member, announcing names of Auditors and details of the dialogue for the Declaration of a Master and/or Treasurer. This is particularly useful for a new Master or at an Election or Installation meeting where the Lodge Business is lengthy or complicated.

Alternative methods of production and distribution of the summons are addressed in Chapter 6.7.

9.2 Minutes

The recording of Lodge proceedings in the Minute Book is one of the Secretary's most important duties. In the event of dispute, audit or a celebration (such as a centenary), the minute book will be subject to close scrutiny.

Rule 177 states "*No Brother shall publish or cause to be published anything which, according to the established principles of Masonry, ought not to be published*". This means that the Secretary should be cautious in recording proceedings in the minutes if they are circulated.

Grand Lodge considers that Minutes are intended to provide the formal record of the business transacted at each Lodge meeting rather than a detailed description.

However, the following information is required by Rule 144 to be recorded in the Minutes:-

- *"The names of all members present at each meeting of the Lodge…"*
- *"…the name and Rank of all visiting Brethren together with the name and number of their Lodge."*
- *"The names of all persons initiated, passed or raised in the Lodge, or becoming members thereof, with the dates of their proposal, initiation, passing and raising or admission respectively, together with their ages, addresses, titles, and professions or occupations."*

In addition to the above stated requirements of the *Book of Constitutions*, the minutes should record the following:-

- Dispensations read in Open Lodge.
- corrections to previous minutes.
- reading of Master's or Grand Secretary's Certificate and additional statement *(Rule 164).*
- brethren appointed or invested as officers of the Lodge.
- all propositions, votes and resolutions.
- record of presentations, declarations and lectures.
- salutations, welcomes, greetings, congratulations, thanks, complaints and apologies.
- reports from Lodge Officers, alms collected.
- issues reported in the Risings.
- any other item included on the Agenda or issues brought to the attention of the Lodge.

The order that the information is recorded in the Minutes should follow the Agenda for the meeting.

With the use of word processing software, the writing up of the minutes can be simplified by making modifications to the minutes of a previous similar meeting or by generating and using a set (library) of standard paragraphs and changing names and dates.

Grand Lodge permits the use of "Loose Leaf" minutes books provided that the pages are firmly affixed and signed on each page by the Secretary or the Master.

Grand Lodge is concerned that the minutes can become too lengthy and provide unnecessary or inappropriate information, particularly related to the description of Ceremonies.

It therefore has stated that minutes should be restricted *"...in so far as they relate to the ceremonies of the three degrees and the Installation of the new Master, to identifying the ceremony, the Candidate and the particular Brethren undertaking the work (if that is not immediately obvious from the offices such Brethren hold)."*

To save time at meetings, Grand Lodge is encouraging Lodges to distribute the minutes with the summons so that they can be pre-read by the members and 'confirmed' rather than read out in full at each meeting.

9.3 Propositions, Ballots and Notices of Motion

9.3.1 Propositions and Ballots

A proposition can be made by any subscribing member of a Lodge in respect of any matter covered by the Rules of the *Book of Constitutions* or the Lodge by-laws.

An Honorary Member who is a Past Master of the Lodge may only propose candidates for initiation or joining but not for any other business.

An Honorary Member who is not a Past Master may neither propose candidates nor any other business.

Every Proposition requires a Seconder and a vote of Lodge Members present and voting, or in some instances a majority of those present. In most instances, a majority in favour is sufficient to carry the proposition. If there is a tie, the Master has a casting vote.

However, there are a number of instances where a majority of two-thirds is required:-

- Removal of Lodges - Rule 141(ii),
- Transfer of Membership on Amalgamation - Rule 165A(c)
- Permanent Exclusion - Rule 181(e)
- Lodge joining another Grand Lodge - Rule 187(ii)
  or where a majority of or three fourths is required:-
- Motion to prevent Installation of Master Elect - Rule 105(b)

If a Proposition is made and seconded and, during the ensuing debate, an Amendment is proposed and seconded, the Master should take a vote on the Amendment first. If the vote for the Amendment is carried then the first proposal is amended accordingly. If the Amendment fails, a vote should be taken on the original proposition.

There are also different periods of notice required to be given to members depending upon the subject of the proposition.

The proposition for candidates for initiation, joining, re-joining or honorary members is made at a Regular Meeting and the vote, that is taken by ballot, must take place at the next Regular Meeting or the proposition lapses. With the ballot, a minimum number of black balls will exclude. (See Rule 165 – Rejection on Ballot).

9.3.2 Notice of Motion

A Notice of Motion is used when there is a major or complex decision to be taken regarding Lodge affairs such as a change in subscription or a relocation of the meeting place, in essence, matters that involve a change in Lodge by laws.

A Notice of Motion for the "Removal of a Lodge" (relocation) requires the Motion to be signed by seven subscribing members of the Lodge. (*Rule 141(i)*)

The Motion is likely to have been the subject of much debate to arrive at a defined proposal. The proposer would present the wording of his proposal to the Lodge as a Notice of Motion, in the Second Rising. The proposer would explain the detail of the Motion. It would not have a Seconder, nor would it be the subject of discussion at this stage.

The summons for the following Regular or Emergency Meeting (Chapter 6.2.3) would state "*Pursuant to notice of motion given on the Summons for the last regular meeting ...Bro. (Name and Craft rank) will propose, and ...Bro. (Name and Craft Rank) will second, that the (...full details of Motion).*

All the brethren will therefore have an equal opportunity to debate the issue and raise any particular matters with the Secretary or the Master before the issue is fully debated and voted on, including any amendments, in Lodge.

9.4 Meetings and Ceremonies

The Secretary's work in respect of Ceremonies of Initiation, Passing and Raising is described in Chapter 7.4 Membership.

9.4.1 Preparation for Election Meeting

Election of Master

The Election and Installation of the Master of a Lodge are of the utmost importance involving many Secretarial Duties.

No brother is entitled by progression or by rank to be Master of a Lodge. It is for the Lodge to select and elect their choice.

For a Warden to have served a 'Full year' in office, he must have been present at the installation meeting for his year of office to qualify, (subject to the exemptions allowed within the Rules). If he is present at neither the Installation for Junior Warden nor for the Installation for Senior Warden, he does not qualify for election as Master.

Prior to the ballot or declaration, either the Master or the Secretary should explain to the brethren that any subscribing member of a Lodge, who is not in arrears with his dues (according to the Lodge's by-laws) and who has served the office of Warden in a regular Lodge for a full year, is eligible for election to the office of Master, with the following provisos.

At the time of the election, the Secretary should be aware that a brother will not be eligible for installation as Master in the following circumstances unless he has the benefit of a Dispensation:-

- no Brother shall continue as Master of the same Lodge for more than two years in succession
- no brother shall be Master of two Lodges at the same time.
- no brother shall become Master if he has not served a full year as a warden in a regular lodge.

If any of the above circumstances exist and after the election a dispensation is refused, Rule 106 – Death or Incapacity of Master Elect will apply.

For a brother to be a Master of two Lodges at the same time the Dispensation is needed from the Grand Master (or District Grand Master if both Lodges are in the same District). Before the election of a Master, the Secretary should determine, whether he is or will become Master of another Lodge during his Mastership and whether he has commitments in another Lodge for a year before and a year after his Mastership as he would be obligated to continue as Master in any Lodge of which he is Master if his successor is not installed.

As a matter of practice a dispensation is hardly ever refused for a second chair - but hardly ever granted for a third.

In most instances, the Senior Warden will be happy to progress and will be elected or declared as Master Elect for the ensuing year. However if this not the case, it is the duty of the Secretary (and other senior Lodge Members) to ensure the smooth transition of Mastership of the Lodge.

The Secretary should be made aware of who in the Lodge is putting himself forward for election as Master. If there is only one nomination for Master Elect in advance of sending out the Summons for the Election Meeting and the Secretary is not aware of any other candidates, the details of the nominated brother shall be included on the Summons for the Election Meeting.

If the nominated brother's name is on the Summons and no brother present at the Election Meeting requests a Ballot, the Master shall declare the nominated brother as Master Elect for the ensuing year. The dialogue of the declaration at the meeting should be similar to :-

WM – "Bro Secretary, have there been any other nominations for the office of Master (or for Treasurer)?"

Sec - "No, Worshipful Master" (N.B. If any other nominations have been received or if a ballot is requested, a formal ballot must be taken).

WM – "Then Brethren, I declare that Bro X has been duly elected as Worshipful Master for the ensuing year and Bro Y has been duly elected as Treasurer for the ensuing year."

An alternative set of words suggested by Graham Redman in his book, "*Emulation Working Today*" is:-

WM – "Bro Secretary, it appears from the summons that Brother ….. is the only Brother nominated to serve as Master for the ensuing year. Has any other Brother subsequently indicated to you that he wishes to be considered?"

On receiving a negative reply from the Secretary, he should ask

WM – "Brethren, neither Brother Secretary nor I have received notice that any Brother wishes to be considered. Does any member of the Lodge wish to call, nevertheless, for a ballot? – (Pause) – Then I declare Bro …… has been duly elected as Master for the ensuing year."

If more than one brother has expressed his willingness to serve, if elected; or if a brother asks for an election; or if the nominated brother's name does not appear on the summons, an election shall take place.

If there is an election for Master, the Secretary should read the names of all brethren who have expressed their willingness to serve but should also inform the brethren that they may enter the name of any eligible brother on the ballot slips. The Brother with most votes becomes Master Elect. In the event of a tie the Master has the casting vote.

It would be prudent of the Secretary to have Ballot Slips available, even in the case of a proposed Declaration, lest a member present requires a Ballot.

Motion to prevent Installation of Master Elect

If not less than two weeks before the Installation Meeting, the Secretary receives a written Notice of Motion that the Master Elect should not be installed, signed by its Proposer and Seconder, together with a separate signed statement giving their reasons, the Secretary shall send a copy of the Motion and the separate statement to the Master Elect.

The Secretary shall then distribute the Summons (or Appendix to the Summons) on which is printed a copy of the proposed Motion (but not the Statement).

If the motion receives three-fourths of the vote on a ballot, the election of Master Elect shall be void and the brethren shall proceed to elect another qualified brother as Master. He shall then be duly installed within five weeks at a Regular or Emergency meeting.

Election of Treasurer

Any subscribing member of a Lodge who is not in arrears with his dues (according to the Lodge by-laws) may be elected as Treasurer. He shall be elected by the members on the regular day of election of the Master and in the same manner.

This means that the same rules, as for the election of a Master, apply to a Declaration if there is only one nomination for Treasurer; and to a Ballot if there is more than one nomination; or if a brother asks for an election; or if the nominated brother's name does not appear on the summons.

Appointment or Election of Tyler

The Tyler must be elected by a show of hands. If it is resolved to elect a subscribing member of the Lodge as Tyler, he shall not be entitled to any emolument.

Many Tylers have held the office for a number of years and it is courtesy to enquire of the Tyler whether he is prepared to continue in office before such election, and to notify him of the result.

9.4.2 Preparation for the Installation Meeting

The Secretary's duties in preparing for the Installation Meeting and assisting the Master Elect in planning his year include:

- Advice on the choice of Lodge Officers if requested.
- Produce a Schedule of Work in Progress to help the Master Elect with planning his programme.
- Ensure Past Master's Collar and Jewel are obtained and engraved for presentation to the Immediate Past Master. (If it is Lodge Custom).
- Ensure that the Master Elect obtains his Master's apron.
- Find out if any Official Visitors are attending from Metropolitan, Provincial or District Grand Office.
- Advise on invitations to brethren from Mother, Sister and Daughter Lodges.
- Provide and get decisions on menus and wines for the year, particularly installation night.
- Determine if Master has any preference for table stationery.
- Enquire if entertainment or Master's Song is required at the Festive Board.

The Secretary should complete the Installation Return Form so far as can be done in advance of the Meeting.

9.5 Lodge Attendees, Visitors and Dining

9.5.1 Attendees and Responses

Whilst it is not the Secretary's role to ensure each member attends the Lodge, it is his duty to ensure that each member receives a summons. He is usually the only regular corresponding Lodge contact with each member. If a member does not respond to the summons it is for one of the following reasons:-

1. The member does not receive the Summons. - In this case the Secretary and the Member need to ensure that the correct postal or email address is being used and that the Secretary's address data base is up to date.
2. The member is waiting, due to personal or business pressures, to see if, he is able to attend or how many visitors he will be bringing.

   All too often the date that this information is known by the member is too late for the Secretary to give the Caterer his required notice for meal numbers. This then entails hurried phone calls and late changes to reported numbers.
3. The member is unable to communicate due to illness, domestic or business pressures. It is on these occasions that a phone call from the Secretary is often most welcome. He can then alert the Almoner, Charity Steward or Mentor as appropriate.
4. The Secretary has not received a response that had been given or sent directly by the member or has been passed to a third party. Failures in communication will always happen.
5. The member has forgotten, not opened the summons or put it in the bin. These are usually, but not always, the less active members.

One might say that only in last circumstance should the Secretary take no action, but even this is not always the case as forgetfulness is not uncommon amongst some of our older members.

After some time as Secretary, the non-attendees, non-responders and late responders will be well known and can be handled accordingly. The action taken by the Secretary is likely to involve a combination of enforcing boundaries, establishing 'regular diners' lists, encouraging co-operation and phoning around.

The minimum work that is required in dealing with the attendance of members and their visitors at each meeting and at the festive board is the following:-

- The Secretary to send out the summons with a reply card
- The member responds saying that:-
  - he is or is not attending
  - has xx visitors and their names and ranks
  - how many will be dining and any dietary requirements.
- Secretary reports any absent officers to the Director of Ceremonies so he can organise substitutes.
- Secretary reports numbers dining to Caterer including any dietary requirements.

It is important that the Secretary sets boundaries such as:

- 'No reply - no meal'
- 'All ordered meals must be paid for - attending or not'.
- 'All active officers will be deemed to be attending unless the Secretary is notified to the contrary'.

Other factors that affect the amount of work each Secretary does are:-

- If the Summons is posted, the scale of packing envelopes is in direct proportion to the size of the membership and the number of meetings.
- The Secretaries of smaller Lodges often need to 'chase' members to fill the offices for ceremonies or achieve minimum dining numbers.
- An increasing number of outside caterers apply long lead-in periods for notification of dining numbers, higher minimum numbers and less flexibility of changed numbers 'on the night'. This puts additional pressure on the Secretary to obtain and firm up numbers well in advance – a task that is not always possible.
- Where a member's subscription includes the cost of meals, it may not go without an element of disharmony if the member is informed on the night that he cannot have a meal because he did not respond.

Using Attendance and Dining Information

The Secretary is obliged to record in the minutes the names of "*...all members present at each meeting of the Lodge, and of all visiting Brethren with the names and numbers of their Lodges and their Masonic ranks.*"

If this information is saved on a data base in conjunction with dining and numbers of visitors, it can be used for a number of purposes.

1. Register of members attending each meeting.
2. Register of members dining with their visitors (to collect dining dues).
3. Data base to determine which members have missed two or three consecutive meetings so that follow-up action may be organised.
4. Data base of attendance for use when considering members for promotion.

9.5.2 Admission and Refusal of Visitors

Visitors to the Lodge are the lifeblood of our meetings but as with all things in Freemasonry, caution is required in admitting Visitors to a Lodge.

All Visitors must either be personally known and vouched for by one of the Brethren present or vouched for after due examination. If necessary, he shall produce his Grand Lodge Certificate and proofs of good standing.

It is the duty of the Junior Warden to examine visitors and the Master to prevent any unqualified Visitor from being received into his Lodge. In practice, the authority and Masonic knowledge of the Secretary is usually called upon to support and advise if any visitor's admittance is in question.

Any Visitor from a different Constitution shall produce his Certificate and show that he complies with the requirements of Rule 125(b). The Master of the Lodge is required to ensure that such a different Constitution is recognised by Grand Lodge. The Secretary is normally asked to make this check.

Every Visitor is subject to the Lodge by-laws during his presence in Lodge. The Master of a Lodge may refuse admission to a visitor "*...of known bad character...*" if the Master believes his presence in the Lodge will cause disharmony.

The Information for the Guidance of Members of the Craft point out that there are "*...Lodges of unrecognised constitutions meeting in England, and care must be taken that their members are not admitted to our meetings*".

9.5.3 Dining

Apart from those Lodges who use a Dining Secretary, it usually falls to the Secretary to organise the Caterers including arranging the selection of menus (via the Master) and sometimes the selection of Wines if ordered centrally.

The Treasurer is responsible for paying the dining charges and gathering the dining fees and the Lodge Committee is responsible for setting the Lodge Dues and Visitors Dining Fee.

However, the Secretary, being the principal correspondent with the Caterer often has to either balance the meal costs to meet the Lodge Dues or advise the Master that his menu selections must be within a set amount.

It is of great help to have a regular diners list, the members of which only notify the Secretary if they are not dining.

It is useful to have a register of diners' and visitors' special dietary requirements.

The Summons, meeting and dining organisation provides the prime contact with all the Members, whether a 'Dining Secretary' is used or not. This 'one to one' contact at each meeting serves as a bond between a Lodge and its Members, alerts the Lodge of sickness or distress and can provide early notice of those members whose attendance is slipping so that Mentoring can be applied.

9.5.4 Table Seating Plans

Many Lodges produce a seating plan at the Festive Board to maintain order. This has a number of advantages including preventing brothers from rushing to the dining room from the Temple and 'tilting' chairs against the table in their favourite location. It also prevents the newer brethren from having to search for an available place and visitors being shuffled around to be near to their host.

In order to satisfy the brethren, the Summons reply slips can include a request as to who the member would like to sit near. Visitors would always be seated as near to their host as practicable.

With the position of the Wardens pre-determined and the Master and most of the top table also generally predictable, the Secretary or Dining Steward can arrange the remaining members and their visitors to achieve the most convivial evening. This is particularly important for the Member who comes to the Lodge alone or rarely, or is a new member.

It is worth re-considering the 'Traditional' dining set up if numbers are low. As an example if twelve are dining, the use of a head table and two sprigs would mean that most of the members or visitors had their backs to each other. Arrangement around a long table would probably prove more convivial.

CHAPTER 10

LODGE MEETINGS

10.1 The Secretary's Role in the Lodge

Having completed the preparation, the Secretary has to ensure that all his efforts are converted into a well run and happy meeting. This involves attending to the following as required:-

1. to have on hand the various reference books, papers and documents necessary to assist him in meeting the range of requests and events that either will or may happen.
2. to see that the planning and preparation is being realised in the Lodge Room.
3. to report on Agenda items to the Lodge.
4. to record Lodge attendees, events and activities.
5. to obtain signatures on forms, documents and correspondence.
6. to manage arrangements relating to the Festive Board.

10.2 Documents, Information and Other Items in Hand

The following lists are intended to remind the Secretary which documents, information and other items are necessary to meet each circumstance in the Lodge.

10.2.1 At every Meeting

- The Warrant of the Lodge
- Attendance Book
- Dispensation if applicable – (e.g. emergency meeting or changed meeting date)
- Minutes of previous meeting for signature by Master

- Spare copies of Summons for Visitors, forgetful brethren and those who are unable to print emailed summons.
- Grand Lodge Certificates or other documents, jewels or collars for presentation.
- List of items and supporting paperwork for the Risings
  - To report the proceedings of Grand Lodge
  - To report on matters concerning Metropolitan, Provincial or District Management
  - To report on Group matters
  - To give notice of propositions for membership and joining
  - To attend to any other business, correspondence, apologies for absence, etc.
- Any document requiring the signature of the Master or other Lodge Officer
- Reference Books and Papers necessary at every meeting
  - *Book of Constitutions* with Updates
  - *Information for the Guidance of Members of the Craft*
  - Lodge By-laws
  - Minute Book
  - Blank Application forms for initiation and joining
  - Metropolitan/Provincial/District Year Book Masonic Year Book
  - Various booklets issued by Grand Lodge

10.2.2 At the Initiation Ceremony

- Candidate's Application/Registration Form
- Letters from other Provincial Grand Secretaries regarding Rule 158 – Other Localities (if applicable).
- *Book of Constitutions, Information for the Guidance of Members of the Craft* and *The Masonic Charities* for presentation to Initiate.
- Lodge by-laws for presentation to Initiate.
- Logbooks or Masonic Information Booklets provided by Metropolitan/ Provincial/District Grand Lodge
- Lodge Centenary or other Lodge information booklets
- Questions and answers for Passing (sometimes provided by Director of Ceremonies or Tyler

10.2.3 At the Passing Ceremony

- Logbooks or Masonic Information Booklets provided by Metropolitan/ Provincial/District Grand Lodge
- Questions and answers for Raising (sometimes provided by Director of Ceremonies or Tyler)

10.2.4 At the Raising Ceremony

- Logbooks or Masonic Information Booklets provided by Metropolitan/Provincial/District Grand Lodge
- Book of Ritual for presentation to newly Raised Brother (if Lodge custom)
- Check candidate has Master Mason's Apron

10.2.5 At the Election Meeting

- Sufficient ballot slips for Master Elect and Treasurer in case Ballot required.
- Dispensation if appropriate – Rule 109.

10.2.6 At the Installation Meeting

- Dispensation if appropriate – Rule 115.
- *Book of Constitutions* for reading of Antient Charges
- *Book of Constitutions* for newly installed Master
- Lodge by-laws for newly installed Master
- Installation Return completed ready for signature by the newly installed Master
- Check Master Elect has a Master's Apron

10.2.7 At a Meeting when there is a Candidate for Joining

- Joining Member's Application/Registration Form
- Valid Certificates of Good Standing from every present and past lodge to which the Candidate does belong or has belonged
- Lodge by-laws for presentation to joining member
- *Book of Constitutions* for presentation to joining member (if from another constitution)
- Confirmation from the Grand Secretary (or the District Grand Secretary as appropriate) that the Grand Lodge under which the Brother was initiated is recognised by the Grand Lodge.
- Declaration Form for joining member to sign (if from another Constitution)
- Lodge Centenary or other Lodge information booklets

It can be seen that to take all the above to each meeting would require a trolley. Providing that the safe keeping of books and documents takes priority, the physical burden may be reduced as follows:-

- Copying information on attendees and visitors required for the minutes from attendance book at the meeting and leaving the Attendance Book in the Lodge Box.

- The Warrant is the responsibility of the Master who sometimes looks to the Secretary to take charge of it. Again, the Lodge Box, if secure and/or insured may be no less safe than in the Master's or Secretary's bag or at their homes.
- Additional copies of the *Book of Constitutions*, by-laws, Application Forms, Lodge and/or Grand Lodge booklets may be kept in the Lodge Box.
- If the Minute Book is 'Loose Leaf' and the minutes are 'Word Processed', the current minutes for signature (and initialling) must be affixed in the Minute Book before signature.
- It is important that the Secretary's information is well ordered or all his best efforts could dissolve into 'fumbling' with papers or missing attending to one of his notes 'on the night'.

10.3 Planning and Preparation in the Lodge Room

Whilst the Secretary cannot predict every eventuality, he will learn very quickly that what he knows and what he has been told sometimes bear little relationship to what actually happens.

It is therefore advisable for the Secretary to arrive at the Lodge Venue in good time in order that he can make spare summonses available, arrange his paperwork, answer any questions from the Master and Brethren and see that all matters for the evening's proceedings are in hand and as expected.

In this way, last-minute changes and events can be dealt with in the most appropriate way in an atmosphere of calmness.

Typical spoilers of the best laid-schemes are:-

- Non-attendance of candidates or officers
- Lost or missing Warrant
- Transport or extreme weather problems
- Allocated Lodge room too big, small, hot or cold.
- No Lodge room furniture, lodge box or Tyler
- Catering issues with room, numbers, service or quality

10.3.1 Non-Attendance of Candidates or Officers

The Secretary will usually have the latest information as to which brethren will be attending each Lodge meeting. He will know this from the responses to the summons, late notifications of absence or attendance with or without visitors, and 'on the night' information from other brethren.

As soon as practicable, and on an ongoing basis, the Secretary should inform the Director of Ceremonies of any offices that need to be filled by acting officers and the brethren who are available.

Even with all this effort, information and intelligence, scarcely a meeting goes by when the predicted number of brethren and visitors all appear on the night.

In most instances, absentees can be substituted but there are a number of exceptional circumstances that are not so easily resolved and can create additional work for the Secretary. Whether in this latter category or not, the Secretary is often consulted on the best course of action.

The absence of a Candidate can be dealt with by having a 'practice' ceremony and the absence of a Brother who was to undertake a significant part of a ceremony may be replaced by substituting a Past Master or Visiting Brother – supported by a good prompter if necessary.

10.3.2 Unexpected Absence of Master Elect for an Installation

The unexpected absence of the Master Elect at an installation meeting is more serious. If one has not heard from him, it would be appropriate to take all possible steps to find out where he is and if he is well.

If he is well and will be late, a decision must be taken whether the meeting can be delayed or not, maybe by juggling the Agenda.

If he cannot make the meeting but still wants to be installed as Master, the Installation can be deferred for up to five weeks, either at the next Regular meeting, if occurring within that period or at an Emergency Meeting within five weeks. If, the Installation takes place within five weeks, the new Master will invest his officers and they will have been deemed to have served a full year in office.

If the installation cannot take place within five weeks, the existing Master must remain in office, appoint the officers that have been selected by the Master Elect, where available, or else select and appoint his own officers.

If the current Master has already served two years in the chair and due to the foregoing rules, he is required to fill the office for a third year, no Dispensation is required.

If becoming Master again would cause him to be the Master of two Lodges, the other Lodge must apply for a Dispensation to enable him to be installed in a second Chair.

If your Lodge is the "Second Lodge", and the dispensation is refused, Rule 106 will apply.

If the current Master is unable or unwilling to sit for a third year then his only recourse is to resign from the Lodge as he holds the office of Master and there is no facility within the Rules for a Master to resign his office. He is obligated to fill the office until a successor is elected and installed in his stead.

If he does resign from the Lodge, Rule 119(a) will apply and the Lodge shall be summoned until the next regular period of election by the Senior Warden, Junior Warden, Immediate Past Master or Senior Past Master as available. In this case an Installed Master will be requested to occupy the Chair to open and close the Lodge and to confer degrees.

In essence, if it is not until the date for Installation that the Master Elect becomes unavailable, there will be no further election. If the current Master either cannot or will not continue the Lodge is to be ruled by Wardens or Past Masters, as above.

10.3.3 Lost or Missing Warrant

Without the presence of a Warrant, it is not possible to open a Lodge Meeting. The Secretary may be called upon to explain the rules and take the necessary action.

The Warrant is placed in the hands of the Master who is responsible for its safe keeping. Whilst it is not the intention that he should keep it in his possession at all times, its safekeeping and production whenever and wherever the Lodge meets is his responsibility.

If the Master is unable to produce the Warrant, the Lodge cannot be opened (Rule 101) *"…nor should any item of business on the Agenda be dealt with and the circumstances giving rise to such a situation should be reported immediately to the proper Masonic authority by the Master"*.

The *"…proper Masonic authority…"* is the Metropolitan, Provincial or District Grand Secretary who should be contacted with the utmost urgency, if necessary by telephone on the afternoon of the meeting, in order that the necessary steps can be taken to enable the Lodge Meeting to take place.

If the Warrant is lost, Rule 103 states *"…the Lodge must suspend its meetings until a warrant of confirmation has been applied for and granted by the Grand Master…"*.

The replacement of a lost Warrant is not undertaken lightly (nor cheaply) so time is normally allowed for thorough searches to take place.

10.3.4 Severe Disruption of Lodge

The Lodge has no power to cancel or adjourn any Regular meeting (Chapter 6.2). Should there be a severe disruption of the Lodge Meeting due to a transport strike, extreme weather problems or bomb alert etc, the meeting may have to be abandoned and the fact recorded in the Minute Book of the Lodge.

10.3.5 Other Issues

Other disruptive issues such as an uncomfortable Lodge Room, shortage of Lodge paraphernalia or issues pertaining to the Festive Board can be anticipated but not foreseen and should be dealt with on an ad hoc basis.

10.4 Report on Agenda Items to the Lodge

The Secretary has a very active role in the Lodge, having to stand and address the Master and the Lodge with regard to about two-thirds of the items on the list of Standard Agenda clauses, (issued by Metropolitan, Provincial or District Grand Lodge) as follows:-

1. To read the Dispensations (if applicable)
2. To inform the Director of Ceremonies/Master of any brethren who have not been appointed or invested.
3. To have Grand Lodge Certificates available for presentation and to instruct brethren where to sign.
4. To read out details of Candidate for Initiation prior to Ballot, and confirm that Rule 158 has been complied with and any associated comments (if applicable).
5. To check that Candidate for Initiation has signed the Declaration Book and report to the Master.
6. To read out details of a joining member (or re-joining member) prior to Ballot.
7. To explain who are the Candidates and procedure for the Election/ Declaration for the ensuing year to the Master and Brethren.
8. To partake in the dialogue with the Master regarding the Declarations of Master Elect and Treasurer.
9. To report that the Tyler has confirmed that he is willing to stand as Tyler of the Lodge.
10. At the request of the Master, to name the brothers nominated as Members of the Lodge Committee.
11. At the request of the Master, to name the brothers nominated as Auditors.
12. To read the Antient Charges to the Master Elect.
13. To be appointed as Secretary.
14. To read out details of an Honorary Member prior to Ballot.
15. To read out Propositions.
16. To report at the First Rising on the Proceedings of Grand Lodge.

17. To report at the Second Rising on matters concerning Metropolitan, Provincial or District Management, to report on Group matters and to give notice of propositions.
18. To attend at the Third Rising to any other business including reporting apologies etc.

10.5 Record Attendees, Events and Activities

The Secretary is to take such notes as will enable him to write up the Minutes of the Meeting. See Chapter 9.2.

10.6 Obtain Signatures as Required

The Lodge meeting is the ideal place to obtain the signature of the Master and other Lodge Officers on forms, documents and correspondence.

It would be better to deal with this matter before the meeting as attempting to recover signatures after the Master and the Brethren have left the Lodge can be tiresome.

It may also useful to remind the Treasurer to complete the details, fill in and obtain second signatures on any cheques that need issuing in the near future. Second signatories must not sign blank cheques.

10.7 Misbehaviour in Lodge

The Secretary should be in the position to advise the Master, if required, when the actions of a Brother (or Brothers) is seen to disturb the harmony of the Lodge. This would be recognised as misbehaviour by the Grand Lodge.

If a Brother disturbs the harmony of the Lodge he shall be admonished by the Master (See Rule 180).

If he persists he shall be censured and/or a vote shall be taken and subject to the opinion of a majority of the members present he shall be excluded for the remainder of the meeting.

If it is deemed appropriate by the Master, the case may be reported to higher Masonic authority.

The consequence of persistent misbehaviour would be to consider exclusion of the Member in accordance with Rule 181.

10.8 Issues Relating to the Festive Board

Most of the Secretary's work in connection with the Festive Board will have been done before the Lodge Meeting. However, the following steps may still need to be taken, either by the Secretary or a Steward acting on his behalf.

Once more, if things are not as expected or required, positive action is more likely to be successful if the issues are raised with the Caterer at the earliest possible moment.

10.8.1 Dining Room Check

Many Masonic Centres have numerous dining rooms of varying quality, size and atmosphere. If a change is required or preferred, due to the attendance of a Senior Official Visitor, handicapped brother or the need of a piano, the change will be effected more easily if several hours notice is given.

10.8.2 Number Check

Most Caterers reasonably require two days' notice of final dining numbers. However, it is not unknown for the Caterer to agree to a reduction of one or two at 'the last minute' without being charged. Notice before the tables are set would help with this.

If there is any doubt as to how many brethren attending Lodge will be dining, a show of hands can be requested.

This gives eleventh hour numbers and enables the manual adjustment of the table plan by stewards, removal of unused place settings and action to avoid brethren sitting alone on a table sprig.

10.8.3 Special Meals Check

There are many different menu requests now due to food allergies, dietary preferences and religious stipulations. A pre-meal check that all the requirements have been met may be considered a wise precaution.

10.8.4 Table Plan

The table plan and place cards can be passed to the Stewards for display and distribution, including any amendments.

10.8.5 Toast List

It is useful for the Secretary to have a copy of the latest Toast List to pass to the Director of Ceremonies. The toast lists are available as a download from the Metropolitan, Provincial or District Web Site.

CHAPTER 11

NON-MEETING RELATED ACTIVITIES

Apart from Lodge Meetings and the preparation for them, the Secretary has to deal with many issues and actions that are not necessarily or specifically Meeting related.

11.1 Correspondence

Whilst the majority of correspondence to a Lodge is addressed to the Secretary it is seldom intended as personal to him, unless, in consequence of which, additional work ensues. Indeed all correspondence has to be dealt with, most communicated, distributed or subject to action and some within critical deadlines.

Correspondence can be received by post, by hand or by email.

A Register of correspondence provides ordered management. If the Register is held on computer, it can assist not only with the recording of information but also with the administration and management of the Lodge.

Correspondence emanates from Grand Lodge, Metropolitan, Provincial or District Grand Lodge, Other Lodges, the Master and members of the Lodge and their families and connections, service providers and suppliers and the general public.

A register of incoming correspondence may include the following:-

11.1.1 General Information

Name of sender	Description of content
Date written	Date posted
Date received	Method Sent

There are occasions when senders back-date correspondence. If this is suspected and of importance, by keeping the envelope and recording the date written, date posted and date received, any claim can be contested, supported by evidence.

11.1.2 Reply Required

Whether reply required	Reply deadline date
Whether response sent	Date response sent
Reply file reference	

The reply reference could include the file name and location on the computer or disk.

11.1.3 Report Allocation

Allocate to 1st Rising	Allocate to 2nd Rising
Allocate to 3rd Rising	Allocate to Lodge Committee
Allocate to other Lodge Business	

Whether or not the correspondence has been answered or subject to action, at the appropriate stage it should be reported to others in the Lodge. By allocating an item to its intended destination, its details can be easily recalled at the relevant time.

11.1.4 Copy of Correspondence

Grand Lodge	Metropolitan, Provincial or District. Grand Lodge
Master	Wardens
Treasurer	Almoner
Lodge Officers	Charity Steward
Past Masters	Lodge Committee
All Brethren	Lodge of Instruction
Individual Brother	

Letters of import need distributing with the required urgency to those to whom the subject pertains or have some other form of interest therein.

11.1.5 Action Required

Whether action required	Description of action taken
Date action taken	Correspondence Concluded
Date Concluded	Remarks

Recording what action is needed, was taken, by whom and when not only concludes the issues raised but safeguards the Secretary.

11.1.6 Alerts

A good correspondence management system could provide alerts or timed reports giving warnings of the following:-

Correspondence not yet concluded
Action Still Required
Reply urgently required (pending deadlines).

11.1.7 Reports

Having been fed with the above correspondence information, it should be possible to obtain reports that sort and filter against any of the above headings giving the following lists:-

Correspondence for Risings	Correspondence by sender
Outstanding correspondence	By date received
Received between dates	Concluded correspondence
Action required	

11.2 Masonic Honours and Promotions

11.2.1 Generally

The issue of Masonic Honours and Promotions is an area of the Secretary's work that requires him to be detached and even-handed initially followed by the dedicated endorsement of an individual.

It is for the Lodge to select those of its members who are deemed worthy for appointment or promotion to Metropolitan, Provincial or District Honours

There is no definitive method of selecting a brother for Honours other than requiring that all available Past Masters (including Country members) should be involved in the decision as to who should be put forward.

The practice of putting forward a brother because it is "...his turn...' is deprecated by Grand Lodge. Honours will only be awarded on merit, based on the contribution a Brother has made, and will continue to make, to his Lodge and to Masonry in general. Fulfilling the necessary selection criteria is more important than seniority.

The first a Lodge hears about honours for any of its Members is receipt, by the Secretary, of the appropriate forms for appointment or promotions from the Metropolitan, Provincial or District Grand Lodge asking for the Lodge's nomination of a Brother for consideration for honours.

A 'Promotions Schedule' could be produced which would track each member and their progress against each category of Honour, indicating when and if each brother became eligible and if appointed or promoted. A matrix could also be produced listing the Lodge Offices held by all Past Masters over previous years.

In the absence of such a schedule a suggested method for selection would be for the Secretary to identify the Brother or Brethren eligible for promotion and produce the following information for each candidate:-

- The number of meetings held and attended in the past five years
- The number and period of non-progressive offices held
- Ritual and other work done in Lodge other than that attributable to offices held.
- Attendance, involvement and offices held at Lodge of Instruction.
- Other Masonic Involvement – particularly Craft & Royal Arch and in the same Province.
- Service or involvement in Masonic Centre or Office
- Community or Charitable activities outside Freemasonry

Honours are less likely to be considered for any Brother who:-

- has held a Non-Progressive Office in Lodge more than ten years
- has been subject to any Masonic disciplinary sanction
- has either ceased membership of a Lodge under Rule 148 or been excluded under Rule 181.

The above information should be readily available if the Secretary maintains a good data base or uses Lodge management software.

This information may be sent to all past masters who, with the benefit of the foregoing information, will be better able to make their selection of who should be put forward, which they must send to the Master in confidence. Those being considered for honours should be excluded from the circulation of their own details.

Details of the selected candidate should be added to the Form in the appropriate boxes along with a narrative summary of his other Masonic and Community activities.

The Form should then be delivered to the Visiting Officer who may review the information with the Master and the Secretary. The Visiting Officer will review the Proposal with the Metropolitan, Provincial or District Executive who will carry it forward.

As there are always likely to be more brethren eligible for promotion than there are appointments to be made, there must be a way of selection.

The selection methods will vary but are likely to include the following:-

- a points system
- weighting those filling certain offices
- the writing style of the brother who submits the form
- the efforts put in by the Visiting Officer
- a combination of all of the above
- factors unknown

If the Secretary himself is eligible, he should arrange for another Brother to collate the views of the Past Masters in putting forward their recommendation.

Whilst the promotion, if granted, is intended to come as a surprise, the gathering of the above information cannot always be done without the involvement of the brother under consideration. The surprise element is not so much in being considered as it is in the having honours awarded.

11.2.2 Types of Promotion

Full details of the required information for submission are available from the Metropolitan, Provincial or District Grand Secretary.

There are three types of honour that can be conferred on a Mason, these being:-

1. London or Overseas Rank
2. London, Provincial, District or Overseas Grand Rank
3. Grand Rank

Honours are not conferred on brethren by the Lodge but by the Metropolitan, Provincial or District Grand Master after receiving submissions of forms and proposals by the Lodge.

1. London or Overseas Rank

   These honours are granted to distinguish Brethren who have not passed through the Chair, who have been a member of the Lodge for at least 10 years and have filled a non-progressive office (Treasurer etc.) for at least seven years.

   It would be unusual if there was more than one brother in a Lodge eligible for this category at any one time.
2. London, Provincial, District or Overseas Grand Rank

   Brethren who have passed through the Chair and remain active in Freemasonry become eligible for these ranks some years after coming out of the Chair. Each Province has slightly different criteria, methods of awarding appointments and promotions and closing dates for submission of Forms, but the general rules are the same and the information as described above is all a Lodge Secretary can provide.

   a. **London Grand Rank**

      London honours are different from Provincial and District honours for a number of reasons.

      Historically, London Masons were managed from within Grand Lodge in Holborn. The various offices appointed by "London Management" were limited to "London Grand Rank" and "Senior London Grand Rank" rather than the 30 or so different ranks awarded in the Provinces and Districts.

      Since the establishment of the Metropolitan Grand Lodge, Brethren can be appointed as Acting Metropolitan Grand Officers. They are then appointed to the appropriate designation (as for Province and District) such as "Metropolitan Grand Standard Bearer".

      At the time of being appointed to their office of Acting Metropolitan Grand Officer they are also appointed to either London Grand Rank or Senior London Grand Rank depending upon the seniority of their Acting Office. There are no "Past Metropolitan Grand Officers".

      One cannot be a MetGL Officer without also being London Grand Rank (either previously awarded or gained coincidental with the appointment of MetGL Office).

      When acting as such, officers holding Acting Rank take precedence over those with LGR and SLGR.

b. **Provincial Grand Rank**
Provincial Grand Ranks can be Acting i.e. taking the office at Provincial Meetings or 'Past' rank (e.g. designated ProvAGDC and PPrAGDC respectively).
Officers holding Acting Rank take Precedence over those holding the corresponding Past Rank.

c. **District Grand Rank**
District Grand Ranks can be Acting i.e. taking the office in District Meetings or 'Past' office (e.g. designated DistAGDC and PDtAGDC respectively).
Officers holding Acting Rank take Precedence over those holding the corresponding Past Rank.

d. **Overseas Grand Rank (Clause 92(a))**
The Honours of Overseas Rank and Overseas Grand Rank may be conferred by the Grand Master on Master Masons and Past Masters respectively, in Lodges abroad not under a District, who are members of the Grand Lodge.

3. Grand Rank
Every Grand Officer is appointed by the Grand Master.
Most appointments to Grand Office will be based on recommendations from or passed through Metropolitan, Provincial or District Grand Masters.
Metropolitan, Provincial or District Grand Lodges each have their own procedures for putting forward recommendations for appointment to Grand Rank.
It is recommended that should a Lodge believe that one of its members should be considered for promotion to Grand Rank, that they approach their Metropolitan, Provincial or District Grand Secretary to determine the best way to go about it.

11.3 Secretary's Expenses

The Secretary is entitled to recover net expenses incurred in the administration of the Lodge. The payment by the Lodge of the Secretary's Annual Subscription is intended to compensate in some way for the many hours expended in administering the business of the Lodge and is not intended to cover out of pocket expenses, (although some Secretaries do treat it as such).

The expenses that the Secretary will incur on behalf of the Lodge include:

- Stationery
- Postage
- Printing Materials
- Room Hire
- Masonic Books and Leaflets
- Regalia and Jewels
- Collars and Engraving of Jewels for Presentation
- Reprinting of by-laws and Centenary Booklets
- Equipment

It is suggested that a detailed running total is kept and submitted for payment at agreed stages, either by value, by meeting or per year.

Distribution of the Summons and correspondence by email considerably reduces the Postage and Stationery element of expenses.

11.4 Compliance

There are a number of items of compliance that the Secretary needs to be aware of lest he encounters them in the course of exercising his duties.

11.4.1 Membership of Quasi-Masonic and other Organisations - Rule 176

A person who has been connected with a quasi-Masonic organisation or an organisation deemed incompatible with the Craft may not be initiated except by leave of the Grand Master.

A Brother who subsequent to initiation becomes connected with such an organisation shall sever his connections or be liable to suspension or expulsion.

11.4.2 Printing or Publishing Proceedings - Rule 177

No Brother shall publish or cause to be published anything which according to the established principles of Masonry ought not to be published. Particular care should be taken in publishing Lodge Websites (See Chapter 12.1.3)

11.4.3 Public Appearance in Masonic Clothing - Rule 178

Wearing any Masonic regalia in any procession, meeting or assemblage at which persons other than Masons are present is not permitted unless a dispensation has previously been obtained.

It should be noted that the Hall Stone Jewel is "…part of your Masonic clothing…" and should not be worn at dinner unless a dispensation has been granted.

11.4.4 Duty to Conform to Law; Reputation of Freemasonry; Breaches of Regulations

It is the duty of every Mason to comply with the laws of the land and not engage in activity likely to bring Freemasonry into disrepute.

A Lodge or Brother offending against any law or regulation of the Craft shall be liable to admonition or suspension.

Details of liabilities ensuing during suspension of Lodges and/or Brethren are given in Rule 179.

11.4.5 Report of Custodial Sentence and other Conduct Likely to Bring Freemasonry into Disrepute - Rule 179a

It is the duty of any Brother sentenced to custodial sentence (immediate or suspended) or to Community Service to report this fact to the Master of his Lodge (or to the Grand Secretary if he is unattached) within 28 days. The Master shall in turn report such sentences to the Metropolitan, Provincial or District Grand Secretary within a similar period.

The Brother who has received such sentences must not attend any Lodge until determination of his case by Masonic Authority has taken place.

It is the duty of every Brother to provide information in relation to a complaint or allegation of misconduct made against him or another Brother or a Lodge.

11.5 Social Meetings

Most Lodges engage in social activities involving its Members and their partners, families, other non-masons and brethren from other Lodges. These are widely encouraged and are largely separate from the Secretary's role.

The social gatherings can include visits to other Masonic Lodges overseas, Luncheon Clubs, 'White Table' events, with or without ladies present; charity fundraising events and 'Ladies Nights' or weekends.

Caution should be exercised at Social Gatherings:-

- if entertaining any non-masons in the Lodge Meeting Room
- not to mention or refer to any Masonic ritual or ceremonies when not in an Open Lodge

- in assuming guests at a social gathering are Masons
- in assuming Masons at a Social Gathering are members of The Grand Lodge.
- not to behave in a manner that would tend to bring Freemasonry into disrepute.

11.6 Lodge History and Centenary Celebrations

Compiling the Lodge History is often delegated to a brother or brethren who do not currently hold the office of Secretary, but it is inconceivable that the information that they have, they need or they generate will not involve discussions and advice from the Secretary.

During the next ten years or so, over a quarter of the Lodges under UGLE will have a significant Anniversary of between 50 – 250 years including 650 Centenaries; 350 anniversaries of 150 Years, seventy-five Bi-Centenaries and fifty 250th Anniversaries. The requirements set down by Grand Lodge for the permission to wear a Centenary Jewel is set down in *Book of Constitutions* Rule 252.

The prime requirement is that there is proof that the Lodge has been in existence, uninterrupted for 100 years or the period for which the Jewel is sought.

A detailed list of procedures and actions necessary to fulfil the requirements of a Centenary Warrant and Anniversary Meeting is available from the appropriate Metropolitan, Provincial or District Grand Secretary.

An assessment of the likely cost of the Centenary to the Lodge should be made, up to ten years in advance, in order that a Lodge Centenary fund may be established in good time.

The future cost is likely to be in the range of £5,000 - £10,000 and will include the following:-

11.6.1 Mandatory Costs

Large Lodge Room
Emergency Meeting Dispensation
Grand Lodge and Province Deputation (10 – 15)
Tyler
Centenary Warrant
Organist

11.6.2 Optional Costs

Entertainment
Centenary Booklet
Centenary Jewels (Future Provision)
Charity Donation
Other Guests of the Lodge (10 – 25)
Centenary Jewels (Members)
Gifts for Guests

11.6.3 Optional Prepayments

Lodge Members Dining.

11.6.4 Three Years before Centenary

The process commences about three years before the Centenary at which time the Lodge should write to the appropriate Metropolitan, Provincial or District Grand Secretary asking them to enquire of the Grand Secretary the date from which the Centenary Warrant, if granted, would take effect..

Once the question has been asked of the Grand Lodge, they will investigate. They may revert back to the Lodge for more information. Ultimately word will be passed down via the Metropolitan, Provincial or District Grand Secretary whether a Centenary Warrant will be issued and when it will take effect – normally 100 years from the Consecration of the Lodge.

11.6.5 One Year before Centenary

At least 12 months before the Anniversary (effective date of the Warrant), the Lodge should submit a formal petition to the MW Grand Master.

If the petition is successful, the Metropolitan, Provincial or District Grand Secretary will determine the protocol. Grand Lodge is unlikely to have involvement in a Centenary but will invariably send a deputation to a Bi-Centenary meeting.

The Lodge's preference has a better chance of being considered if it is not a Monday, Friday or Saturday and does not fall immediately prior to meetings of Grand Lodge or Metropolitan/Provincial/District Grand Lodge.

The deputation will consist of Senior Grand Officers and/or Metropolitan/Provincial/District Grand Officers.

11.6.6 6-9 Months before Centenary

Secretary to attend meeting with Metropolitan, Provincial or District Grand Lodge to discuss Agenda, Toast List, Wine Taking and Top Table Seating Plan.

11.6.7 6-8 Weeks before Centenary

Reminder sent from Metropolitan, Provincial or District Grand Lodge of information required.

11.6.8 4-6 Weeks before Centenary

Four Copies of Lodge History for use of:-

- Guest of Honour who will propose Toast to Lodge
- Chaplain who will give Oration
- Librarian at Grand Lodge
- Metropolitan/Provincial/District Grand Lodge

Draft of Summons, Toast Lists and other relevant Documents should also be sent to Metropolitan, Provincial or District Grand Lodge, as should three copies of the biographical details of current Master, Brother who organised meeting and Brother who wrote Lodge History.

11.6.9 On the Night

- 5:15 pm Lodge Opens
- 6:15 pm Lodge Closes
- 7:00 pm – 7:15 pm Dine
- 9:00 pm – 9:15 pm Guest of Honour leaves, if he wishes

CHAPTER 12

THE WAY FORWARD USING NEW TECHNOLOGIES

It is not intended that this Chapter tries to anticipate future developments in technology. Instead it is intended to be a snapshot of where we are now and from whence we have come in order to give some inkling of the global effect of the rate of change, how it affects us at an individual level and is likely to impact in the future.

12.1 Looking Back

Thirty years ago, (two years before the IBM PC was launched), one could buy an Apple II personal computer for £2500 (about £7,500 in today's money) It had a 1 MHZ processor 48K ram, two 143k floppy disk drives and a monochrome text screen that would show 40 characters wide by 24 rows deep. At that time there was no mouse and no Microsoft Windows.

The Apple II ran the first spreadsheet, a text based program called Visicalc that was 64 columns wide by 256 rows deep. The Apple II also had very basic word-processing and data base programs and was a very powerful tool for its day.

Back in 1980 there was 'Telex' ticker tape but there were no commercial fax machines, no portable computers, no mobile telephones, no text messages, no commercial emails, no Internet, no GPS navigation.

12.2 Where We Are Now

In 2010, for the equivalent of one-twentieth of the cost of the Apple II, one can buy a new PC (Dell Vostro) with 800MHZ processor (800 times as fast), 3073MB ram (65,500 times as powerful) and 320GB hard drive (Over 1 million times as much storage) with a 22" high definition (1680 x 1050) flat screen.

If you want to be really adventurous, for £4,000 (just over half of the price of the Apple II at today's prices) you can buy a Personal Supercomputer that is about 250 times faster than the average PC today (over 1.6 million times faster than the Apple II). Very good for analysing MRI Scans in minutes rather than days – or maybe Provincial Promotions!

Today fax machines (how did businesses manage without them?), are becoming obsolete due to scanning and emailing of documents.

There are 4.1 billion mobile phones world wide with Global coverage via satellites. There are about 40 million mobile phones in the UK which send 2 billion text messages per week, with the number rising at 30% per year.

There are about 200 billion emails worldwide per day, of which 70% are spam. The internet is used by 44 million people in UK, 72% of the population.

The main Internet search engine, Google, was founded 11 years ago and now receives nearly 300 million 'hits' per day, two-thirds of the total internet searches.

If you 'Google' for the following items, the resulting number of search hits are:-

	Million		**Million**
Freemasonry	1.85	Masonic	5.71
Tax	316	Death	419
Religion	238	Politics	275
Text Message	271	SMS	334
Computers	791	Software	1,140
Phone	988	Mobile	1,270
Twitter	1,460	Blog	3,000
TV	2,250	News	2,990
Internet	1,800	Web	3,390

The reason for including these figures is to indicate the impact and the scale of the burgeoning forms of communication.

We are inundated with jargon and acronyms and a completely new "txtg" language. On the plus side, you can 'Google' or look up 'Wikipedia' for any term of which you are unsure and are likely to discover its meaning and a lot more besides.

12.3 Wireless Communication

Development in wireless electronic communication is essential as demand is increasing exponentially. This is due to:-

- the mounting numbers of mobile-phone and wireless-system users, which could easily double in the next decade to 50% of the world population

- the ever-increasing change to wireless data transfer
- the escalating quantity and types of data transmitted.

New wireless technology will be widely used for internet access on computers as well as for cell phone communications. Customers in areas which have strong coverage will be able to use it for home broadband connections which do not require any cabling to their homes.

It can also be used for accessing the internet on the move without having to be in a wireless hotspot such as those offered by some coffee shops, airports and libraries.

We are moving towards a wireless technology environment where all our pieces of electronic equipment can communicate with each other via radio signals rather than by lengths of wire or fibre optic cable.

At a simple level this will include wireless remote controls, but the technology now includes secure and sophisticated connections to multimedia and the safe transfer of immense quantities of data. The clever bits are in the encrypting, transmission, receiving and decrypting. The only wire required is for the power to boost the batteries in your computer or phone and their peripherals.

With wireless connections, users can access telephone, voice and text messages, Internet, GPS maps, business intranets and video conferencing, World and business news updates, information searches for anything or everything, radio and TV broadcasts, films, games or other entertainments.

All of the above can equally be received and viewed on the latest 'BlackBerry' or 'I-Phone' handsets as well as with a laptop computer.

One scenario would be that you can be sitting on a train going to Manchester, open your laptop or I-Phone and look up live flight arrival times from New York, send a text or voicemail to your son giving the arrival time as he is driving to meet your friends at the airport, (he is using his satnav to guide him door to door which also has a 'hands-free' phone and is giving him live traffic details), you can either speak to or send a text message to your friend on the plane and speak on video-phone/laptop webcam to your wife to confirm arrangements. You can then check your own train arrival time on-line, respond to your emails, look at the latest news headlines and financial news. All of this within about fifteen minutes and with no wires.

12.4 Hardware

Computers have doubled in power every two years for the past thirty years and current developments indicate a step change. Computers are also better value now than they have ever been.

Computers and Mobile Telephones of every sort comprise the hardware. Mobile phone technologies include I-Phone, Blackberry and others that have wireless links to the Internet and computer networks.

12.5 Software

The communications systems are the means of carrying the information. Software (or programs) is the means by which we use the computers and communications to perform functions.

Software can be computer operating systems (XP, Vista or Windows 7), emails, word processing, spreadsheet, data base, publishing or bespoke programs.

12.5.1 Emails

The growth of emails has been exponential. They are ubiquitous, pervasive and invasive. One email was sent in 1971 and now there are 200 billion per day.

It is only over the past 5 years that Metropolitan, Provincial and District offices have adopted email as the prime form of communication with Secretaries.

The following observations relating to emails are subjective and doubtless others have better and worse experiences:-

- An email is generally less formal than a letter.
- There is a tendency to use first names in addressing the recipient.
- The email's form is often conversational or even casual.
- There tend to be more spelling and grammatical mistakes than in letters. This is largely due to less care being taken in reading something on screen than a printed document.
- Punctuation and capitals (upper case) text often seem to be used in a random way.
- It is easy to adopt a 'scattergun' approach with information, as adding an additional person to the copy list is 'just a click away'.
- It is relatively easy to send unintended information, especially if modifying a previously sent email.
- It is relatively easy to send an email or copied documents to the wrong person or 'copy in' people who should not receive it.
- Once the 'Send' button has been selected, it is normally 'too late'!
- Follow-up corrections are quite easy to send.

- Spam is a pain and can be dangerous. It can contain offensive material or viruses or it can be an important communication that has been incorrectly channelled into the Spam basket.
- Emails are an extremely convenient way of communicating, both with individuals and especially with groups.
- Emails are an instant form of communication delivering news, questions and answers, documents and pictures in a fraction of the time taken for traditional post.
- Emails should be used with the caution required of a medium that has the capability of sending your written word for the world to see, 20 seconds after the idea of what you wanted to say first came into your head.

12.5.2 Lodge Websites

An increasing number of Lodges are developing their own websites. Grand Lodge have published a paper "Guidance for Members of the Craft and Royal Arch on the use of the Internet and World Wide Web for communicating and informing". It includes a clearly defined policy to prevent breach of Rule 177 – Printing or Publishing Proceedings.

The paper includes "Suggested content of a Lodge or Chapter Website" and "Password protected area".

It stresses that no personal names, details or photos can be included without the written permission of **all** individuals concerned.

It also states that there should be no advertising or commercial links and specifically directs that no mention or links to the website designer should be included.

Lodges should submit the proposed content of any websites for approval by the Grand Secretary before they are published on the World Wide Web. If approved, the website can carry the Grand Lodge charter mark.

Lodge Websites generally give details as follows:-

Home	Welcome Page
Lodge History	Potted history of the Lodge
Associated Lodges	Mother, sister and daughter Lodges
Officers & Meetings	List of Current Lodge Officers Calendar of Meetings, L of I and Events
Lodge Activities	Details of past social events with pictures
Charity	Details of current and past Charities that are supported by the Lodge and Freemasonry

About Freemasonry	What Freemasonry is about, links to other Masonic literature and information and contact details.
Contact Us	Contact details of non-progressive Lodge officers and of Chapter Scribe E.
Links	Links to Grand Lodge, Province and other associated Masonic organisations.
Members Log-in	Members page to download L of I details, summons and other information and respond regarding dining and visitors.
Chapter Pages	Link to Chapter website or details of Chapter, meeting dates and contacts.

If a Lodge wants to set up a website, help is often available from the Provincial Office, or other Lodges who have already set up their own websites. These can be found by looking for links in the List of Lodges from the Provincial Website.

Some Provinces actually provide templates on which each Lodge can enter their details, the server on which the website can be held and email addresses for the Secretary of each Lodge.

12.5.3 Intranets

An intranet is a private computer network, usually within a business or other organisation that uses Internet technologies to securely share any part of its information or operational systems with its employees or members. Lodges could use intranets for their 'Member's Room' activities by giving Members password access to a section of the website.

12.5.4 SMS Text Messages

SMS text messaging is the most widely used data application on the planet, with 3 billion active users, or 74% of all mobile phone subscribers sending and receiving text messages on their phones.

A whole new shorthand text dictionary has come into existence that you can find on the internet if interested.

"Texting" is used most extensively by the younger generation who punch messages to each other, with their thumbs, at tremendous speed. Regrettably, some of the text abbreviations are creeping into emails and letters.

12.5.5 Twitter (Description from Wikipedia)

"Twitter is a free social networking and micro-blogging service that enables its users to send and read messages known as tweets. Tweets are text-based posts of up to 140 characters displayed on the author's profile page and delivered to the author's subscribers who are known as followers. Senders can restrict delivery to those in their circle of friends or, by default, allow open access. Users can send and receive tweets via the Twitter website, Short Message Service (SMS) or external applications. While the service costs nothing to use, accessing it through SMS may incur phone service provider fees."

Basically this is continuous conversation of not more than 25 words at a time, by text. One might think that it is not the sort of thing that would really catch on – but look, it has 1.46 billion search hits on Google!

12.5.6 Blogs (Description from Wikipedia)

"A blog (a contraction of the term "weblog") is a type of website, usually maintained by an individual with regular entries of commentary, descriptions of events, or other material such as graphics or video. Entries are commonly displayed in reverse-chronological order."

This is a way that anybody from Tom Thumb to Prime Ministers can regularly express their views to the World, supported by their own evidence (or not) – unedited. Those who read the 'blog' can add their comments.

If the blog is not of general interest it will not get read. If it is, word will quickly spread and it could be read by millions.

12.5.7 Wikipedia

Wikipedia is a multilingual, web-based, free-content encyclopaedia project. It is a very useful tool to find out anything about everything (or everything about anything) from the meaning of a word or phrase to advice on how to set up your own blog site.

Looking up Masonic terms gives answers and also links to Masonic research sources such as Quatuor Coronati and Masonic Bodies including UGLE.

The English-language version of Wikipedia has over 3 million articles and nearly 18 million pages. However, this is the tip of the iceberg as the links from its pages each lead to much more information, e.g. one link on one page to Quatuor Coronati accesses all of its Masonic Research references and all QCCCs web links to other sources. (http://www.wikipedia.org/)

12.6 How all this Technology helps the Secretary

12.6.1 Generally

As indicated in the Introduction "The role of the Lodge Secretary can best be defined as one of communicating Information, Knowledge and Wisdom relating to Organisations, People and Events. "

The various chapters of the book clearly identify the information relating to people, lodges and meetings as data that has to be captured, processed and communicated within a framework of rules.

It therefore follows that any tools that will assist in making the data easier to access, amend, update, sort, filter, report and communicate to the brethren and Masonic authorities, must be of benefit.

If, within that process, the format of the data is generated in a standard format to suit Metropolitan, Provincial or District Grand Lodge requirements, the tasks of both the generator and the receiver of the information must benefit.

If the book of rules can be integrated with the data and is aligned to the Lodge Management process, this benefits the Lodge and the Province by reducing the learning curve when becoming Secretary and by bringing each and every relevant rule to the attention of the Secretary at the time when he is carrying out his duties.

The technologies that can deliver these tools are the computer and the communications systems together with appropriate software.

12.6.2 Software

There is a wide range of software that has been written to utilise the above technologies. These or generically known as Word Processing, Spreadsheets and Data Bases. These can all be used effectively to assist the Lodge Secretary.

It must always be remembered that the best software in the world will not produce satisfactory results unless the right data is entered and kept up to date. This applies to whatever software is used. Even when tasks are carried out manually, if the wrong information is used the wrong results ensue.

It must also be remembered that without data, software is a blank sheet, even if sometimes a very clever blank sheet.

The amount of time to produce the templates, spreadsheets and data base programs should not be underestimated, nor should the amount of time taken to input all the current and historical data.

Data has to be clean. If you want to sort by address or surname, all the surnames have to be in the same column. If you want to search by a word or a name, it has to be spelt correctly – every time.

If two, three or four different programs are used, it must be remembered that multiple entry of the same data will occur and it is probable that data mismatches will happen, such as – updated changes of address and/or dates only changed in one place.

12.6.3 Word Processing

Meeting Minutes

The Minutes of the Lodge Meeting can be produced with Word Processing software. In most instances, it should be possible to take a copy of previous minutes from a similar meeting and to modify them.

Be careful to print out all updated documents and carefully read the printed version. This is because errors and omissions are more easily missed when reading from the screen.

An alternative to modifying previous minutes is by creating a template, with or without standard clauses, and using that as a base document.

It is possible to create a small library of standard clauses for each ceremony. The clauses can be allocated a short reference code such as [Opening Para 1 or 'OP1'] etc. The clauses can then be called up using the abbreviation and arranged in order with details entered into the blanks.

The source of the standard clauses could be copied from previous minutes or may be available from the standard minutes provided by Metropolitan, Provincial or District Grand Secretary.

Provincial Forms

One can prepare a template for each of the Forms required for passing to the Metropolitan, Provincial or District Grand Lodge. Whenever the form is required, the appropriate details can be filled into an empty template, or a previously completed form can be modified.

The Annual Returns and Installation Returns are required to be returned on the Grand Lodge forms which are sent from Metropolitan, Provincial or District Grand Lodge. It is likely that these forms will be available in electronic format within the next couple of years, but until then they must be completed manually.

It is possible to produce a Template for the Installation Returns - LP&A4 but the Annual Returns are not suitable for Word Processing due to their format, their size and their self duplicating qualities.

Address Labels

Address Labels may be produced from Word Processor by using a Label 'wizard'. If the basic member information is kept on a spreadsheet, any changes of address may need amending twice.

Summons

The Summons can be produced in a Word Processing program, the first time by copying a previous printed Summons. However, replicating a summons can be a complex task and should not be attempted to a deadline by someone who is unsure of what they are doing.

The difficulties will arise around

- graphics - incorporating Lodge crest, scanning, overall layout
- fonts - different size, style, colour and compression of fonts
- margins - centralising and positioning all the information
- columns - aligning columns of names, addresses and dates
- modifications - the Summons has to accommodate basic data changes for subsequent summonses each month and at installations.
- pagination - the set-up for printing has to accommodate printing pages 1 and 4 together and 2 and 3 together etc.
- weight/quality of paper – this gives the Summons its 'feel'.

If the Summons has previously been produced at a Print Shop, it may be on 150gsm paper/card and may have embossing. The average desktop printer will not deal with that weight of paper nor embossed paper.

The options are to send your completed Summons out to the Print Shop for printing or to reduce the weight of paper to about 110gsm.

If in difficulty, it is suggested that help is sought from someone who is familiar with desktop publishing.

Once all the above issues have been resolved, editing the summons for each meeting is reasonably straightforward but has to be done meticulously.

12.6.4 Spreadsheets

Spreadsheets are the most fantastic tools for listing, sorting, filtering, reporting and cross-referencing information.

If preferred, spreadsheets can be used to generate the templates for the forms and for producing address labels. However, it is not recommended to attempt the summons on the spreadsheet as the setting-out may go awry if a different size of font is required on the same line on an adjacent page.

Member Details

Members' details including names and addresses can be usefully held on a spreadsheet. The labels sheet can be linked into the sheet containing the list of member's names and addresses.

Once again care has to be taken with multiple data entry and data mismatch, particularly if using an inherited spreadsheet from your predecessor and you are unsure as to exactly how it works.

Other information such as a matrix for Masonic Honours, Offices Held by Members or the Lodge Work Programme can also be produced with a spreadsheet. Data sorting, filtering and graphics make the reports easy to understand and interesting.

12.6.5 Data Bases

A data base is the most effective tool in which to enter member and meeting details. Each record can be properly coded, referenced and indexed with each field classified.

Relationships between data held in different tables can be created to facilitate the writing of comprehensive reports.

With the correct coding and relationships, and the entry of full sets of data, all the reports required can be generated from the data base. Alternatively data can be linked, copied or exported to spreadsheet or word processing programs for other reports or Lodge management purposes.

12.6.6 Bespoke Software

There is software available for table planning, suitable for the Festive Board. It can deal with any table configuration or table shape, individual's or group's seating preferences, and produce plans, schedules and place cards. If the Secretary is also the dining steward, it is a piece of software he should not be without.

The author has to declare an interest at this point in also being the author and the owner of The Complete Lodge Secretary computer program. It was written during a first stint as Secretary in 1994 when facing many of the foregoing issues for the first time.

The program has been through two reincarnations since then and the program was the reason that the author was asked to write this book.

The Complete Lodge Secretary computer software is a bespoke data base program that dynamically incorporates the *Book of Constitution* Rules and *Information for the Guidance of Members of the Craft.*

The Complete Lodge Secretary holds all the data, entered only once. It deals with most of the items covered in this book and guides the Secretary through each circumstance as it occurs, cross referencing and on occasions being dependent upon compliance with the *Book of Constitution* Rules.

It contains many standard reports and enables the user to download the data into proprietary Word Processing, Spreadsheet or Data Bases to facilitate exceptional reports or for other Lodge management purposes.

12.7 Leading Edge Technology

As a general statement, try to avoid the leading edge technology until it has bedded in and is seen as free from teething problems. Search the Internet before taking the plunge (Google - 'Problems with ...') and you will soon see if there are any issues you should avoid.

Appendix
Schedule of Book of Constitutions Rules referred to

Clause	Description		Book Section	Page
9	Qualification of Past Masters		6.3.10	67
47	To whom business papers and reports to be transmitted		2.2.1	19
74	Power to summon Officers and Brethren		6.4	68
90	Dispensation to confer degrees at short intervals		5.1.4; 9.1.3	47; 108
92(a)	Overseas Grand Rank		11.2.2	136
101	A Lodge not to act without a Warrant		6.3.2; 10.3.3	58; 126
103	Warrant lost or withheld		10.3.3	126
104	Officers of a Lodge	]	2.2.2	22
104(a)		]	2.2.1; 9.1.1	19; 107
104(c)		]	2.2.1; 2.2.3	19; 24
104(d)		]	2.2.1; 9.1.1	19; 107
105	Election and Installation of Master.	]	3.8; 6.3.10	66; 67
105(a)		]	2.2.1; 6.3.2	19; 58
105(b)		]	2.2.1; 9.3.1	19; 112
105(b),(c)		]	6.3.2	58
106	Death or incapacity of Master Elect		2.3.6; 5.2.2; 9.4.1; 10.3.2	27; 48; 113; 125
107	Continuation in office of Master		6.3.2; 9.1.3	58; 108
108	Postponement of installation of Master		9.1.3	108
109	Qualification of Warden for Master's Chair		6.3.2; 9.1.3	58; 108
111	Master's obligation		6.3.2	58
112	Election of Treasurer		9.1.3	108
114	Master responsible for observance of laws		6.3.2	59
115	Master's period of office/Master of more than one Lodge		5.1.4; 6.3.2; 7.3.1; 9.1.3	47; 59; 79
116	Appointment and Investiture of Officers		6.3.2	59
117	Proprietor of Meeting Place		6.3.2; 9.1.3	59; 109
118	Brethren to attend summonses		6.3.2; 6.4	59; 68
119(a)	Death of Master and other contingencies		8.2.4; 10.3.2	101; 126
120	Removal of Officers		6.3.2; 6.3.9	59; 66
121	Vacancies in regular Offices		6.3.9	66
122	Official visitation of Lodges		6.3.2	59
125	Admission of Visitors	]	6.3.2	59
125(b)		]	9.5.2	119
126	Refusal of admission to visitors		6.3.2	60
127	Disqualification to visit		7.4.6; 8.1	95; 98
136	By-laws		2.2.3	23
138	Master to receive copy of By-Laws		6.3.2	60
139	Prohibited days for Meetings		6.3.2; 9.1.3	60; 109
140	Emergency Meetings		6.3.2; 9.1.3	60; 109
141	Removal of Lodges	]	6.1.1; 6.3.2; 9.1.3	53; 60; 109
141(i)		]	9.3.2	112
141(ii)		]	9.3.1	112
142	Removal of Lodges for one meeting		6.3.2; 9.1.3	60; 109
143	Property, Furniture, Jewels, Books, Papers of a Lodge		4.1; 6.3.2	33; 60
144	Minutes		2.2.1; 2.2.2; 6.3.2; 9.2	20; 22; 61; 110
145	Lodge Subscriptions		6.3.2; 6.3.7; 7.4.7	61; 66; 96
146(i)	Annual Return of Members		2.2.1	20

INDEX